T0089282

FAN FARE

KATE McMILLAN

PHOTOGRAPHY BY
LAUREN BURKE

weldon**owen**

CONTENTS

GAME ON

It's game day! Whether it's the regular season or the Super Bowl, opening day or a must-win game seven, or just poker night with the neighbors, it's an occasion that calls for casual entertaining—and heaping plates of crowd-pleasing, crave-worthy food and plenty of refreshing drinks. That's where *Fan Fare: Game-Day Recipes for Delicious Finger Foods, Drinks, and More* comes in. With more than 60 recipes to choose from, it's your playbook for the menu. A mix of classic bar-bite staples and modern riffs on tailgate standards, these are your go-to recipes for an easygoing gathering. Many of the recipes gathered here are for foods that can be easily eaten with a fork or fingers and can be made in advance, giving you more time to watch the tipoffs and touchdowns and relax with your guests.

WARM-UP WITH NIBBLES

Get the party started with bowls of crunchy-salty nibbles, such as the oh-so-addictive Sweet & Spicy Nuts (page 45), Maple-Bacon Popcorn (page 49), and Party Chex Mix (page 48). Serve trays of finger foods like Stuffed Mushrooms (page 58) and Classic Deviled Eggs (page 74), which are tailor-made for filling and have been party favorites for decades. Jalapeño Poppers (page 57) are newer to the party scene but a bar-food staple; here, they're packed with bacon as well as cheese. For something salty and chewy, bake a batch of soft pretzels—you'll find five options here for this beloved ballpark standard: pretzels with mustard, pretzel bites with parmesan and garlic or cinnamon and sugar, pretzel sticks with ale cheese sauce, and pigs in a pretzel—always a surefire party hit (pages 52–55). For the crowd who prefers their snacks crisp and fresh, serve a platter of seasonal crudités with a bowl of ranch dip (page 32).

BRING ON THE HEARTIER FOOD

No big-game viewing is complete without buffalo wings, and for good reason: These all-American bar-food favorites are ideal finger food—just be sure to supply plenty of napkins with them. Try the Sweet Jalapeño Wings, Honey-Sesame Wings, or the more traditional Spicy Buffalo Wings (pages 68–69). Small-plate bites that can double as dinner fare include Hanger Steak Sliders (page 83), which pair perfectly with Garlic-Parmesan Fries (page 25).

You can raise your game by serving a few more-sophisticated bites such as the Tandoori Chicken Kebabs (page 66), aromatic with coriander, turmeric, cumin, and saffron; or make an array of flatbreads (pages 60–61), with toppings ranging from corn, tomato, and basil for your vegetarian guests to caramelized onion and sausage for the meat-eaters. Vegetarian and meat-topped versions of stuffed potato skins here, too.

QUENCH YOUR THIRST

When you're hosting, the last thing you want to do is spend all of your time making individual cocktails for each guest. Batch cocktails for a crowd work best (served from pitchers), so mix up pitchers of drinks beforehand, especially favorites such as Classic Margarita (page 22), or Bloody Mary (page 92) and Mint Mojito (page 93). Set out and refresh a small ice chest, supplied with a scoop, within arm's reach of the drinks (plan on about a half pound of ice per person; more during warm-weather months). Be sure to have plenty of beer (perfect with buffalo wings), wine, and nonalcoholic drinks on hand as well.

MAKE IT SELF-SERVE

Game day calls for casual entertaining—no place cards, candlelight, or centerpieces required. When it comes to laid-back gatherings, nothing beats a buffet table: The food can be arranged on platters and set out on a table, sideboard, or kitchen island, and guests can chat as they serve themselves, creating a warm, convivial atmosphere. Arrange the buffet with plates at one end and silverware at the other, and be sure to set out a stack of large napkins so that guests can put their plate on their lap comfortably.

Serve this decadent dip with sturdy tortilla chips or soft corn tortillas for scooping up the crispy sausage and melted cheese. To make it vegetarian-friendly, substitute 1 cup (5 oz/ 155 g) coarsely chopped sautéed mushrooms for the chorizo. If you like it spicy, stir in ½ cup (3 oz/90 g) fire-roasted poblano chile strips with the tomato just before serving.

QUESO FUNDIDO SERVES 6

Preheat the oven to 350°F (180°C).

In a skillet over medium heat, brown the chorizo, breaking it up with a wooden spoon and stirring occasionally, until cooked through, about 6 minutes. Using a slotted spoon, transfer to a plate. Pour off all but about 1 tablespoon of fat from the skillet and add the onion. Sauté, stirring occasionally, until soft, 6–7 minutes. Turn off the heat and stir in the reserved chorizo, the tomato, and 1 tablespoon of the cilantro.

In a shallow baking dish, spread half the cheese across the bottom of the dish. Top with the chorizo mixture and finish with the remaining cheese. Bake until the cheese melts, 4–5 minutes. Top with the remaining cilantro and serve with the tortillas or chips for dipping.

4 oz (125 g) fresh Mexican chorizo, casing removed

½ white onion, chopped

1 Roma tomato, chopped

2 tablespoons fresh cilantro, chopped

1 lb (500 g) Monterey jack cheese, shredded

Small flour or corn tortillas, or tortilla chips

With its bubbly browned top and rich flavor, this old-style party dip is always a hit. To save time the day of the party, make the crostini up to 2 days in advance and store them in a lock-top plastic bag at room temperature. For a gluten-free alternative, serve jicama sticks.

HOT ARTICHOKE-PARMESAN DIP SERVES 6

1 thin French baguette

3 tablespoons olive oil

Kosher salt and freshly ground pepper

1 can (14½ oz/415 g) artichoke hearts, drained well

1 cup (250 ml) mayonnaise

1 cup (4 oz/120 g) freshly grated Parmesan cheese

1 tablespoon Worcestershire sauce

Hot pepper sauce, such as Tabasco

Preheat the oven to 375°F (190°C).

Cut the baguette into ¼-inch (6-mm) slices and place in a single layer on a baking sheet. Brush the tops with oil and season with salt and pepper. Bake until golden brown, about 12 minutes. Set aside.

In a food processor or blender, combine the artichoke hearts, mayonnaise, Parmesan, Worcestershire sauce, and a few drops of hot pepper sauce and process until finely chopped. Spoon the dip into an ovenproof dish and bake until warm and bubbly, about 20 minutes. Serve right away, with the crostini for dipping.

Turn up the heat in this game-day staple with more chile, cool it down with extra sour cream, or build seven layers by adding chopped green or red onion and sliced black olives. If possible, use a clear glass dish so the colorful layers are visible.

MEXICAN
FIVE-LAYER DIP SERVES 4–6

In a small nonreactive bowl, stir together the tomatoes, onion, half of the cilantro, the oil, 1 tablespoon of the lime juice, and the jalapeño. Season with salt and pepper and set aside.

In another bowl, mash the avocados until very smooth. Stir in 1 tablespoon lime juice and the remaining cilantro and season with salt. Set aside.

In a third bowl, stir together the sour cream, chili powder, and the remaining 1 teaspoon lime juice, and season with salt. Set aside.

In a saucepan over medium heat, gently warm the refried beans, stirring often.

In a serving dish approximately 10 inches (25 cm) in diameter and 2 inches (5 cm) deep, use a rubber spatula to spread the refried beans across the bottom of the dish. Wiping the spatula after placing each layer, spread a layer of the sour cream mixture on top of the beans, followed by layers of guacamole, cheese, and finally the salsa. Serve with chips for dipping.

3 Roma tomatoes, chopped

¼ cup (1 oz/30 g) chopped white onion

½ cup (½ oz/15 g) loosely packed fresh cilantro leaves, chopped

2 teaspoons olive oil

2 tablespoons plus 1 teaspoon fresh lime juice

1 teaspoon finely chopped seeded jalapeño chile

Kosher salt and freshly ground pepper

2 ripe avocados, pitted and peeled

1 cup (8 oz/250 g) sour cream

1 teaspoon chili powder

1 can (16 oz/500 g) refried beans

¾ cup (3 oz/90 g) shredded Cheddar cheese

Tortilla chips

Roasted Tomato Salsa
Page 21

Caramelized
Onion Dip
Page 42

ADD SPICE

Charred tomatoes give smoky flavor to salsa. Minced chipotle chiles are another good smoky-flavored addition.

TRY FRESH HERBS

Dried herbs are the status quo in classic ranch dip, but using fresh herbs instead adds a more mellow and nuanced flavor.

Ranch Dip
Page 32

Taqueria Guacamole
Page 20

A SIMPLE SWAP
Substitute chopped steamed spinach for the artichoke and you'll have another of the best party dips around.

Homemade Ketchup
Page 100

Hot Artichoke-Parmesan Dip
Page 16

EASY GO-TO DIPS

Blue Cheese Dip
Page 100

Perfectly ripe, silky avocados are key to nailing this simple yet sublime recipe. They are ready to eat if they give slightly to gentle pressure. To ripen firm avocados, slip them into a paper bag, add a banana or apple, close the top, and leave for 1–3 days, checking them daily.

TAQUERIA GUACAMOLE SERVES 6

3 ripe avocados, halved and pitted

3 tablespoons chopped fresh cilantro

Juice of 1 lime

1 or 2 dashes of hot pepper sauce, such as Tabasco (optional)

Kosher salt and freshly ground pepper

Scoop the flesh from the avocados into a bowl. Using a potato masher or a large fork, smash the avocados until mostly smooth. Stir in the cilantro, lime juice, and hot sauce, if using. Season with salt and pepper and serve right away. To store, cover the bowl tightly with plastic wrap so that the plastic is touching the guacamole and refrigerate for up to 1 day.

CHUNKY GUACAMOLE Pit, peel, and cut 3 avocados into ½-inch (12-mm) cubes and place in a bowl. Add 2 Roma tomatoes, cut into small dice; 3 tablespoons finely chopped red onion; ¼ cup (⅓ oz/10 g) chopped fresh cilantro; the juice of 1 lime; and 1 small jalapeño chile, seeded and minced. Gently toss. Season with salt and pepper and serve right away.

AVOCADO CREMA Scoop the flesh from 1 avocado into a small bowl and mash with a large fork until creamy and smooth. Stir in ¼ cup (2 oz/60 g) Mexican crema or sour cream and 1 tablespoon fresh lime juice. Season with salt and serve.

The deep smoky flavor of this classic partner to tortilla chips comes from charring the tomatoes and jalapeño under the broiler. If good-quality fresh tomatoes are not in the market, substitute 1 can (14½ oz/455 g) fire-roasted tomatoes.

ROASTED TOMATO SALSA SERVES 6

Preheat the broiler. Line a baking sheet with aluminum foil.

Cut the tomatoes in half lengthwise and arrange on the prepared pan, cut side down. Place the jalapeño, garlic, and onion on the pan so everything is in a single, uncrowded layer. Drizzle with the oil. Slip under the broiler about 6 inches (15 cm) from the heat source and broil, turning the vegetables once and rotating the pan as needed, until the vegetables are charred all over, about 5 minutes per side. Remove from the oven and let cool.

When the vegetables are cool enough to handle, seed the jalapeño and peel the garlic. Combine the tomatoes, jalapeño, garlic, onion, and cilantro in a blender or food processor. Process until well combined with no large chunks, but still with plenty of texture. Add the vinegar and pulse to combine. Season with salt. Serve right away or store in an airtight container in the refrigerator for up to 1 week.

1 lb (500 g) Roma tomatoes

1 jalapeño chile

3 cloves garlic, unpeeled

½ white onion, quartered

2 teaspoons olive oil

⅓ cup (½ oz/15 g) loosely packed fresh cilantro leaves, chopped

1 teaspoon red wine vinegar

Kosher salt

Some mixologists swear by Cointreau and some by Grand Marnier. Some prefer silver tequila and others gold. Simply put, there are lots of recipes for the beloved margarita. Pour this classic version into a pitcher and ready a tray of salt-rimmed glasses for do-it-yourself service.

CLASSIC MARGARITA SERVES 6

Coarse sea salt, preferably Maldon

1 lime wedge

Crushed ice

1 cup (250 ml) silver tequila

⅓ cup (80 ml) orange liqueur, such as Cointreau, triple sec, or Grand Marnier

⅓ cup (80 ml) fresh lime juice

Lime slices for garnish

Pour a thin layer of salt onto a small plate. Moisten the rims of 6 tumblers with the lime wedge. Working with one glass at a time, dip the rims into the salt to coat them evenly.

Fill a pitcher half full with ice. Add the tequila, orange liqueur, and lime juice. Stir to mix, then serve with the glasses alongside. Offer lime slices to add as desired.

BLOOD ORANGE To the tequila and ice, add 1 cup (250 ml) fresh blood orange juice, 1 cup (250 ml) triple sec, and ¼ cup (60 ml) fresh lime juice. Stir to mix. Pour into the prepared glasses, garnish with thin wheels of blood orange, and serve.

WATERMELON Make a watermelon purée: In a blender, combine ¾ cup (4 oz/125 g) cubed watermelon, 1½ teaspoon simple syrup, and a dash of fresh lemon juice. To the tequila and ice, add the watermelon purée, ¾ cup (180 ml) fresh lime juice, ¼ cup (60 ml) St. Germain elderflower liqueur, and ¼ cup (60 ml) simple syrup. Stir to mix. Pour into the prepared glasses, garnish with charred or fresh lemon wedges, if desired, and serve.

Oven fries are easier and better for you than their deep-fried kin. Here, sweet potato wedges are treated to a no-fuss coating of olive oil, salt, and pepper and served with a creamy dip. Choose a flavorful sweet potato variety, such as Garnet, Jewel, Nugget, or Beauregard.

SWEET POTATO OVEN FRIES SERVES 6

2 ½ lb (1.25 kg) sweet potatoes, well scrubbed

2 tablespoons olive oil

Kosher salt and freshly ground pepper

½ cup (4 oz/125 g) crème fraîche

1–2 teaspoons Sriracha

Position a rack in the upper third of the oven and preheat to 450°F (230°C).

Trim the ends from the sweet potatoes. Cut in half lengthwise and place, cut sides down, on a work surface. Using a sharp knife, cut each half lengthwise into wedges ½ inch (12 mm) wide. Place the wedges in a large bowl, drizzle with oil, and toss to coat evenly. Season well with salt and pepper. Place the wedges in a single layer on a large baking sheet, allowing ample space on all sides to ensure even cooking. Bake until golden and tender when pierced with a knife, about 50 minutes.

Meanwhile, in a small bowl, mix the crème fraîche and Sriracha until blended.

Serve the fries with the Sriracha crème fraîche for dipping.

SAGE & GARLIC In a small bowl, combine 1 tablespoon olive oil, 1 teaspoon chopped fresh sage, and 1 clove minced garlic. Spoon atop the hot sweet potatoes and toss to coat.

PARSNIP Substitute parsnips in place of the sweet potatoes and cook as directed. If desired, sprinkle with flaky sea salt (such as Maldon) and chopped fresh dill before serving.

The secret to great French fries—creamy on the inside, crisp on the outside—is to fry them twice, first at a relatively low temperature and then at a slightly higher one. Here, those perfect fries are made game-worthy by tossing them with cheese and garlic. To spice them up, substitute a small spoonful of minced jalapeño chile for the parsley.

GARLIC-PARMESAN FRIES SERVES 4–6

Place the potatoes in a bowl of cold water and set aside.

Pour the oil into a heavy-bottomed pan to a depth of at least 3 inches (7.5 cm) and warm over medium-high heat until it reaches 300°F (150°C) on a deep-fry thermometer.

Drain the potatoes and lay on a plate lined with paper towels, using extra towels to blot dry. Line another plate with paper towels. Working in batches, fry the potatoes for about 4 minutes (there shouldn't be any color on the potatoes), and then, using a wire skimmer or slotted spoon, transfer to the prepared plate. Raise the oil temperature to 375°F (190°C) and, working in batches if necessary, fry the potatoes again. Cook just until golden brown, about 2 minutes.

Using the wire skimmer, return the fries to the towel-lined plate for a few seconds to drain the excess oil, then transfer to a mixing bowl. Add the butter, garlic, Parmesan, and parsley and gently toss. Season generously with salt and serve.

2 russet potatoes (about 1½ lb total weight), peeled and cut into ¼-inch (6-mm) matchsticks

Vegetable oil for deep-frying

1 tablespoon butter, melted

7 cloves garlic, minced

3 tablespoons finely grated Parmesan cheese

½ cup (½ oz/15 g) loosely packed fresh parsley, chopped

Kosher salt

Sriracha Crème Fraîche Page 24

Garlic-Parmesan Fries Page 25

A FUN WRAP

For a casual touch, serve fries or homemade potato chips in cones made of parchment paper.

BAR FRIES

Sweet Potato Oven Fries Page 24

Parsnip Oven Fries
Page 24

ADD SOME KICK

A swift shot of hot
sauce or a liberal dose
of shredded cheese
elevates fries from
plain to primo.

Many would find it downright lonely to watch the game without a big plate of nachos at hand. There is no right or wrong when it comes to toppings, which is good news, as everyone seems to have a favorite. Here, you can swap in shredded chicken for the beef, pintos for the black beans, and pepper jack for the Cheddar.

PARTY-PERFECT NACHOS SERVES 4–6

In a frying pan over medium-high heat, brown the ground beef, breaking it up with a wooden spoon, until cooked through. Pour off all but about 2 tablespoons of the cooking fat. Stir in the chili powder, cumin, and ¾ teaspoon salt and continue to cook for 1 minute. Set aside.

In a saucepan over medium heat, melt the butter. Add the flour and whisk constantly for 1–2 minutes. Slowly whisk in the milk. When the milk begins to bubble, add the cheese a handful at a time, stirring constantly with a wooden spoon. Remove the cheese sauce from the heat and season to taste with salt.

Arrange the tortilla chips in a shallow serving dish. Pour the cheese sauce over the chips and top with the ground beef, black beans, tomatoes, red onion, and jalapeños. Serve with sour cream, salsa, and guacamole on the side.

1 lb (500 g) ground beef

1 tablespoon chili powder

1 tablespoon ground cumin

Kosher salt

2 tablespoons butter

2 tablespoons all-purpose flour

2 cups (500 ml) whole milk

2½ cups (12 oz/350 g) shredded Cheddar cheese

1 bag (14 oz/500 g) tortilla chips

1 can (15 oz/470 g) black beans, drained and rinsed

2 tomatoes, chopped

¼ small red onion, thinly sliced

⅓ cup (2½ oz/70 g) sliced jalapeño chiles

Sour cream, salsa, and guacamole, for serving

When a party calls for more upscale fare, serve this elegant snack with flavors from the Asian pantry. Ginger, sesame, soy, chile, and lime juice heighten the fresh taste of the tuna, while the wonton chips deliver a welcome crunch and wasabi cream adds subtle heat.

TUNA CRISPS WITH WASABI CREAM SERVES 6

FOR THE WONTON CRISPS

12 wonton wrappers, halved diagonally

Asian sesame oil for brushing

FOR THE WASABI CREAM

½ cup (4 oz/125 g) sour cream

2 tablespoons heavy cream

1½ teaspoons prepared wasabi paste

1 tablespoon fresh lemon juice

1 teaspoon low-sodium soy sauce

Kosher salt

1 lb (500 g) sushi-grade tuna fillet, well chilled

1½ tablespoons low-sodium soy sauce

1½ tablespoons Asian sesame oil

2¼ teaspoons fresh lime juice

1 jalapeño chile, finely minced

¾ teaspoon peeled and minced fresh ginger

1 tablespoon minced chives

To make the wonton crisps, preheat the oven to 350°F (180°C). Line a baking sheet with parchment paper. Arrange the wonton triangles in a single layer on the prepared baking sheet and brush lightly with sesame oil. Bake until crisp and golden, 6–8 minutes. Let cool.

To make the wasabi cream, in a bowl, stir together the sour cream, heavy cream, wasabi paste, lemon juice, soy sauce, and ¼ teaspoon salt. Let stand at room temperature to allow the flavors to blend until you are ready to serve.

Using a very sharp knife, trim away any sinew or skin from the tuna fillet. Cut the tuna into ¼-inch (6-mm) cubes and place in a bowl. Add the soy sauce, sesame oil, lime juice, jalapeño, and ginger and stir gently to combine. Use right away or cover and refrigerate for up to 1 hour.

To serve, place the wonton crisps on a platter and divide the tuna equally among them. Sprinkle evenly with the chives, drizzle with the wasabi cream, and serve.

Fried food is always best served right away, so make this ketchup in advance—its heady aroma and deep flavor are the perfect complement to sweet fried onions. If the party date sneaks up on you, spice up good-quality store-bought ketchup with Sriracha sauce instead.

SHAVED ONION RINGS WITH SMOKY KETCHUP

SERVES 4–6

Cut off the tops of the onions. Peel, then cut in half lengthwise. Cut crosswise into very thin slices. Place the slices in a nonreactive bowl and pour the buttermilk over the top. Let stand at room temperature, stirring a few times, for 1 hour.

Meanwhile, make the ketchup: In a heavy-bottomed pan, combine the tomato purée, brown sugar, vinegar, garlic powder, smoked paprika, pepper flakes, and onion powder. Place over medium-high heat and bring to a boil. Reduce the heat to low and simmer, stirring occasionally, until the sauce reduces and thickens, about 1 hour. Season to taste with salt and let cool. Transfer to a small serving dish to use now, or cover and store in the refrigerator for up to 10 days or freeze for up to 1 month.

In a shallow bowl, stir together the flour, 1 tablespoon salt, 1 teaspoon black pepper, and the cayenne.

Line a plate with paper towels. Pour the oil into another heavy-bottomed pan to a depth of 4 inches (10 cm) and warm over medium-high heat until it reaches 375°F (190°C) on a deep-fry thermometer. Grab a handful of the onions, allowing the excess buttermilk to drip back into the bowl, transfer to the flour mixture, and toss gently to coat. Gently shake off any excess flour from the onions and carefully add them to the hot oil. Fry until golden brown, 3–4 minutes. Using a wire skimmer or slotted spoon, transfer the onion rings to the prepared plate and season immediately with salt. Repeat to cook the remaining onions. Serve with the ketchup on the side for dipping.

2 large yellow onions

2 cups (500 ml) buttermilk

FOR THE SMOKY KETCHUP

1 can (15 oz/425 g) tomato purée

1 tablespoon firmly packed brown sugar

¼ cup (60 ml) cider vinegar

⅛ teaspoon garlic powder

¼ teaspoon smoked paprika

¼ teaspoon red pepper flakes

¼ teaspoon onion powder

Kosher salt

2 cups (8 oz/250 g) all-purpose flour

Kosher salt and freshly ground black pepper

¼ teaspoon cayenne pepper

Canola oil for deep-frying

Give this ranch dip a contemporary upgrade with fresh garlic, shallot, and parsley, or go old school with the seasonings and it will still be delicious. Spiralized russet and sweet potatoes fried to a crisp golden brown are great for scooping up the thick, tangy dip.

SPIRALIZED POTATO HAYSTACK WITH RANCH DIP SERVES 4

FOR THE RANCH DIP

½ cup (125 ml) mayonnaise

½ cup (125 ml) low-fat buttermilk

1 tablespoon minced fresh flat-leaf parsley or 1 teaspoon dried parsley

1 teaspoon minced shallot or ½ teaspoon onion powder

1 minced garlic clove or ½ teaspoon garlic powder

Kosher salt and freshly ground pepper

Chopped fresh dill for garnish, optional

Canola oil for deep-frying

2 russet potatoes, peeled and ends trimmed

2 sweet potatoes, peeled and ends trimmed

Kosher salt

To make the ranch dip, in a bowl, combine the mayonnaise, buttermilk, parsley, shallot, garlic, ½ teaspoon salt, and ¼ teaspoon pepper. Stir until blended. Taste and adjust the seasonings. Transfer to a serving bowl and set aside until ready to serve, or cover and refrigerate for up to 3 days. Sprinkle with fresh dill just before serving, if desired.

Fill a wide, deep, heavy-bottomed pot two-thirds full with the oil and warm over medium-high heat until it reaches 350°F (180°C) on a deep-fry thermometer. Line a plate with paper towels.

Meanwhile, using the fine shredder blade of a spiralizer, spiralize the russet potatoes, stopping every 3–4 rotations to cut the strands. Spread out the potatoes on a baking sheet and pat with paper towels to absorb any excess moisture. Repeat to spiralize the sweet potatoes.

Working in batches, deep-fry the russet potato, stirring occasionally with a wire skimmer or slotted spoon, until crispy and golden brown, 4–6 minutes per batch. Using the skimmer, transfer the fries to the prepared plate and season with salt. Repeat to fry the sweet potato, replacing the paper towels as needed. Stack the potatoes on a serving platter and serve with the dip.

There's no need to order pizza once you master these individual deep-dish pies. Each one supplies 2 to 3 bites of perfect, cheesy pizza. Make them ahead, underbaking by 5 minutes, and store in a plastic bag in the refrigerator or freezer; rewarm in a 300°F (150°C) oven until the crust is golden and the filling is warmed through, 5–10 minutes.

PROSCIUTTO, SPINACH & TOMATO DEEP-DISH MINI PIZZAS MAKES 12 MINI PIZZAS

To make the dough, in a food processor, combine the flour, cornmeal, yeast, sugar, and salt and pulse to mix. With the motor running, add the water and oil in a steady stream, then pulse until the dough comes together in a rough mass, about 12 seconds. If necessary, sprinkle with 1–2 teaspoons water and pulse again until a rough mass forms. Let rest for 5–10 minutes.

Process the dough again for 25–30 seconds, steadying the top of the processor with one hand. The dough should be tacky to the touch but not sticky. Transfer the dough to a lightly floured work surface and knead to form into a smooth ball. Place in a large oiled bowl, turn to coat with oil, and cover with plastic wrap. Let rise in a warm place until doubled in bulk and spongy, about 2 hours.

Place a rack in the middle of the oven and preheat to 450°F (250°C).Brush the bottom of each cup in a 12-cup muffin pan with oil. Punch down the dough, turn out onto a lightly floured work surface, and shape into a smooth cylinder. Cut the dough in half. Let one half rest for 10 minutes; reserve the other half for future use. (Store reserved dough in a lock-top plastic bag. Refrigerate for up to 1 day or freeze for up to 1 month; bring to room temperature before using.) Cut the dough into 12 equal pieces. Roll each piece into a 5-inch (13-cm) round. Fit a dough round into each prepared muffin cup. The dough should extend about ¼ inch (6 mm) over the top of each cup.

Spoon 1 tablespoon pizza sauce into each dough cup and season with salt and pepper. Fill each cup evenly with tomato, spinach, and prosciutto, then top with another tablespoon of pizza sauce and the shredded cheese. Bake until the pizzas are golden brown on the bottoms and the cheese is melted, 12–14 minutes. Let cool for 5 minutes, then serve.

FOR THE PIZZA DOUGH

3¾ cups (15 oz/450 g) bread flour, plus more for dusting

⅔ cup (3 oz/75 g) medium-grind cornmeal

1 package (2¼ teaspoons) quick-rise yeast

1½ tablespoons sugar

1 tablespoon kosher salt

1½ cups (350 ml) warm water (110°F/43°C), plus more as needed

Olive oil for greasing

1½ cups (12 oz/350 g) store-bought pizza sauce

Kosher salt and freshly ground pepper

1 large tomato, chopped

2 cups (20 oz/60 g) fresh spinach leaves, chopped

3 oz (90 g) thinly sliced prosciutto, chopped

1 cup (4 oz/125 g) shredded mozzarella cheese

All you need for this show-stopping party snack is a high-quality artisanal loaf, a trio of easy-to-source ingredients, and a hot oven. If you like, experiment with different ingredients, such as Cheddar and jalapeño chile, Gorgonzola and crisp bacon, or Fontina and cooked sausage.

CHEESY OLIVE PULL-APART BREAD SERVES 4–6

1 round loaf artisanal bread

1½ cups (6 oz/180 g) shredded Gruyère cheese

½ cup (2½ oz/70 g) kalamata olives, pitted and coarsely chopped

⅓ cup (½ oz/15 g) loosely packed fresh flat-leaf parsley leaves, chopped

¼ cup (2 oz/60 g) butter, melted

Preheat the oven to 350°F (180°C).

Using a long serrated knife, make cuts in the bread about 1 inch (2.5 cm) apart, being careful to not cut all the way through and leaving about ½ inch (12 mm) on the bottom. Rotate the bread so that you can make cuts in the opposite direction, again 1-inch (2.5-cm) apart.

In a bowl, stir together the cheese, olives, and parsley. Using your hands, stuff the cheese mixture between the cuts, working in both directions. Place the loaf on a baking sheet and drizzle the butter all over the top. Cover with aluminum foil and bake for 15 minutes. Remove the foil and continue to bake until the cheese is melted and the top of the bread is golden brown, about 10 minutes longer. Transfer to a serving dish and serve.

Those who find the arresting aroma of just-cooked bacon irresistible will find it impossible not to indulge in these sweet and salty bite-sized "chips." Serve them like potato chips and have a stack of napkins on hand. You may never be satisfied with plain old bacon again.

MAPLE-BACON "CHIPS" SERVES 6

12 thick-cut slices applewood-smoked bacon

2 tablespoons pure maple syrup

½ teaspoon coarsely ground black pepper

Preheat the oven to 400°F (200°C).

Cut the bacon crosswise into 2½-inch (6-cm) pieces. Spread the bacon pieces out in a single layer on a large rimmed baking sheet.

Bake until the bacon is barely crisp and browned, 15–20 minutes. Carefully drain off and discard the fat from the baking sheet. Brush 1 tablespoon of the maple syrup over the bacon strips and sprinkle with half of the pepper. Return to the oven and bake until glazed and shiny, about 2½ minutes. Remove from the oven and, using tongs, turn the bacon slices over. Brush the other sides with the remaining 1 tablespoon syrup and sprinkle with the remaining pepper. Bake again until glazed and shiny, about 2 minutes longer.

Transfer the bacon to a serving platter. Let stand 2–3 minutes (the bacon will firm up and become extra-crispy). Serve warm.

HONEY BACON Substitute honey in place of the maple syrup.

SPICY BACON Sprinkle both sides of the bacon slices with ground cayenne pepper or chipotle chile powder after sprinkling with the black pepper.

Sweet and salty, crisp and supple, these little treats are surprisingly addictive. Make them ahead if you like, as they are equally good served warm or at room temperature. If just out of the oven, these stuffed appetizers are molten hot, so let them cool a bit before serving.

BACON-WRAPPED DATES SERVES 12

Bring a saucepan three-fourths full of water to a boil over high heat. Drop in the bacon slices, reduce the heat to medium, and simmer for 5 minutes. Drain and dry on paper towels.

Position a broiler pan 4 inches (10 cm) below the heat source and preheat the broiler. Soak the toothpicks in water for at least 30 minutes.

Cut each bacon slice in half crosswise. Stuff each date with about ½ teaspoon of the cheese, wrap a strip of bacon around each one, and secure with a toothpick. Arrange on a rimmed baking sheet.

Slip under the broiler and broil, turning once, until the bacon is crispy and the cheese is bubbling, about 5 minutes. Transfer the dates to a serving platter and serve hot.

12 slices applewood-smoked bacon

12 wooden toothpicks

24 Medjool dates, pitted

3 oz (90 g) Cambozola cheese or other blue cheese

Here, a half-hour dip in a spice-laced brine gives the shrimp a flavor boost, and poaching the bacon for a few minutes guarantees it will cook up crisp on the grill. You can assemble the skewers and refrigerate them a couple of hours in advance and then set them over the fire after your guests arrive.

BACON-WRAPPED SHRIMP SERVES 4–6

Using the tip of a small knife, cut a shallow groove along the back of each shrimp, exposing the dark vein. Lift out the vein with the knife tip and discard. Add the shrimp to the brine, cover, and refrigerate for 30 minutes.

Prepare a charcoal or gas grill for direct grilling over high heat. Brush and oil the grill grate. If using wooden skewers, soak them in water for at least 30 minutes.

Bring a saucepan three-fourths full of water to a boil over high heat. Drop in the bacon slices, reduce the heat to medium, and simmer for 5 minutes. Drain and dry on paper towels.

Remove the shrimp from the brine and discard the brine. Pat the shrimp dry with paper towels. Wrap a half slice of bacon around the shrimp. Slide the wrapped shrimp onto a skewer, piercing it through the middle and securing the bacon. Repeat with the remaining shrimp and bacon.

Place the shrimp on the grill and cook, turning once, until the bacon is a little crispy and the shrimp turn creamy white, 3–5 minutes per side.

Slide the shrimp off the skewers onto a platter. Serve right away.

24 large shrimp in the shell, about 1 lb (500 g) total weight, peeled with tail segment intact

Basic Shrimp Brine (page 101)

6–8 metal or wooden skewers

12 thick-cut slices applewood-smoked bacon, halved

Slowly caramelizing the onion updates this retro dip, giving it an unmistakable homemade flavor. If possible, make it a day or two in advance so the flavors have time to develop and meld. To change up the chips, use sweet potatoes in place of the Yukon golds.

POTATO CHIPS WITH CARAMELIZED ONION DIP SERVES 4–6

FOR THE ONION DIP

3 tablespoons olive oil

1 large yellow onion, quartered, and thinly sliced

Kosher salt and freshly ground pepper

1 cup (8 oz/250 g) sour cream

¼ cup (60 ml) mayonnaise

1½ teaspoons Worcestershire sauce

½ teaspoon garlic powder

¼ teaspoon celery salt

1 lb (500 g) Yukon gold potatoes, peeled

2 qt (2 l) canola oil for deep-frying

Kosher salt

To make the onion dip, in a frying pan over medium-high heat, warm the olive oil. Add the onions, season with salt and pepper, and sauté, stirring often, until soft, about 8 minutes. Reduce the heat to low and continue to sauté, stirring occasionally, until the onions are caramelized, about 25 minutes. Let cool.

In a bowl, stir together the onion, sour cream, mayonnaise, Worcestershire sauce, garlic powder, and celery salt. Season with salt and pepper, cover with plastic wrap, and refrigerate while you make the potato chips.

Using a mandoline or a sharp knife, very thinly slice the potatoes into chips and place in a bowl of cold water.

In a large heavy-bottomed pan over medium-high heat, warm the canola oil until it reaches 350°F (180°C) on a deep-fry thermometer. Drain the potatoes and lay on a plate lined with paper towels, using extra towels to blot dry. Line another plate with paper towels.

Working in batches, fry the potatoes until golden and crisp, about 5 minutes. Using a wire skimmer or slotted spoon, transfer the chips to the prepared plate and season generously with salt. Continue to fry the remaining potatoes in batches. Let the potato chips cool before serving alongside the onion dip.

This easy recipe should come with the warning "Caution—highly addictive." When you put this tasty snack on the table, be sure to have plenty of ice-cold beer within reach. You can prepare the nuts up to a week in advance and store them in an airtight container.

BEER NUTS SERVES 8–10

3 cups (15 oz/470 g) raw peanuts

½ cup (4 oz/125 g) sugar

Flaky or coarse sea salt

Preheat the oven to 300°F (150°C). Line a baking sheet with aluminum foil and coat with nonstick cooking spray.

In a heavy saucepan over high heat, combine the peanuts, sugar, and ⅓ cup (80 ml) water and bring to a boil. Continue to cook, stirring often, until all of the liquid has evaporated and the mixture is pasty, 20–25 minutes.

Spread the peanuts in a single layer on the prepared baking sheet, breaking up clusters, and season generously with salt. Bake, stirring once, until deep brown, 30–35 minutes. Remove from the oven, season again with salt, and serve.

What sets these enticing bar nuts apart from their many competitors is the addition of piney, aromatic rosemary. If a friend is hosting the get-together, pack this portable snack in a cellophane bag, tie it with raffia or a ribbon, and tote it to the party as a game-day gift.

SWEET & SPICY
NUTS SERVES 15–20

Preheat the oven to 350°F (180°C).

Combine the nuts in a large bowl and toss to mix well. Spread in a single layer on a rimmed baking sheet. Toast in the oven, stirring once or twice, until light golden brown, about 10 minutes.

In the same bowl, stir together the rosemary, brown sugar, salt, cayenne, and melted butter. Add the warm nuts and toss to coat. Serve warm. When the nuts are cooled, store in an airtight container at room temperature for up to 1 week.

¼ lb (125 g) *each* peeled peanuts, cashews, Brazil nuts, hazelnuts, walnuts, pecans, and unpeeled almonds, or 1¾ lb (875 g) assorted unsalted nuts

2 tablespoons coarsely chopped fresh rosemary

2 teaspoons firmly packed dark brown sugar

2 teaspoons kosher salt

½ teaspoon cayenne pepper

1 tablespoon unsalted butter, melted

Sweet & Spicy Nuts
Page 45

Party Chex Mix
Page 48

BOOST FLAVOR

Add mix-ins such as citrus
zest, grated cheese, or other
seasonings to popcorn while
it's hot out of the pan.

Chili-Lime
Popcorn
Page 49

Beer Nuts
Page 44

*Maple Bacon
Popcorn
Page 49*

CRISPY BAR SNACKS

MAKE IT SALTY

Flaky sea salt such as Maldon, or a smoky or spiced salt, adds inimitable flavor to plain chips.

*Potato Chips
Page 42*

Sports fans have a hankering for sweet-salty snack mixes. You can dress up this basic formula as you like, trading in plain or flavored bagel chips for the crackers and pumpkin seeds for some of the nuts and adding a handful of dried cranberries or dried cherries for extra sweetness and a splash of hot pepper sauce for a touch of heat.

PARTY CHEX MIX SERVES 12–15

¼ cup (2 oz/60 g) unsalted butter

1½ tablespoons Worcestershire sauce

2 teaspoons sugar

1 teaspoon seasoned salt,
such as Lawry's

½ teaspoon onion powder

¼ teaspoon garlic powder

4 cups (6 oz/180 g) Chex cereal,
in any combination of wheat,
rice, and/or corn chex

½ cup (2½ oz/75 g) mixed nuts

½ cup (2½ oz/75 g) bite-sized pretzels

½ cup (2½ oz/75 g) bite-sized Cheddar
crackers, Cheddar cracker sticks, or
Cheddar goldfish crackers

Preheat the oven to 250°F (120°C). Put the butter in a shallow baking dish and set in the oven until melted. Stir in the Worcestershire sauce, sugar, seasoned salt, onion powder, and garlic powder until blended. Add the cereal, nuts, pretzels, and crackers and toss gently but thoroughly to coat with the seasoned butter.

Spread out the cereal mixture evenly in the dish and bake for 45 minutes, stirring every 10 minutes. Let cool. Serve right away, or store in an airtight container for up to 1 week.

Fast and easy for the cook and always popular with guests, popcorn offers plenty of variety. Here are three variations that deliver big flavor, but don't be shy about exploring other creative combinations, such as shaved chocolate and grated orange zest, brown butter and rosemary, or Cheddar cheese and hot pepper sauce.

POPCORN FOR EVERYONE SERVES 4–6

In a large heavy-bottomed pan with a tight-fitting lid over medium heat, warm the oil. Add the popcorn and cover. Leave the pan untouched until you hear the first few pops, then shake the pan and continue to cook, shaking the pan every 20 seconds or so, until the popping slows down considerably, about 6 minutes. Transfer the popcorn to a large bowl.

Toss the popcorn while it's still hot with one of the flavor combinations below:

CHILI LIME In a large bowl, stir together 2 tablespoons melted butter, 1 tablespoon lime zest, and 1½ teaspoons chili powder. Add the hot popcorn, toss, and season generously with salt.

RANCH In a large mixing bowl, stir together 2 tablespoons *each* melted butter and finely grated Parmesan cheese; ½ teaspoon *each* onion powder, dill weed, and salt; and ¼ teaspoon garlic powder. Add the hot popcorn and toss.

MAPLE BACON In a frying pan, fry 5 thick-cut slices bacon until crisp. Crumble the bacon and reserve 2 tablespoons of the grease. Use the bacon grease to pop the popcorn. In a large bowl, stir together the bacon, 1 tablespoon plus 1 teaspoon pure maple syrup, 1 tablespoon Sriracha, and 1 tablespoon melted butter. Add the hot popcorn, toss, and season generously with salt.

2 tablespoons canola oil

½ cup (3 oz/90 g) unpopped popcorn

When the homely squid is coated and fried to a crunchy golden brown, it becomes one of the most appealing of all seafood snacks, especially when paired with homemade marinara sauce seasoned with red pepper flakes. Be sure to let the oil return to 350°F (180°C) between batches to guarantee crisp, tender calamari.

FRIED CALAMARI WITH SPICY MARINARA SERVES 4–6

To make the spicy marinara, in a saucepan over medium-low heat, heat the olive oil and garlic until the garlic softens and is fragrant but not browned, about 3 minutes. Stir in the tomatoes, oregano, and pepper flakes. Bring to a simmer over medium heat, then reduce the heat to medium-low and continue to simmer, uncovered, until slightly thickened, about 10 minutes. Remove from the heat and keep warm.

Meanwhile, pour the canola oil into a large, heavy saucepan to a depth of 3 inches (7.5 cm) and warm over high heat until it reaches 350°F (180°C) on a deep-fry thermometer. Preheat the oven to 200°F (95°C). Set a large wire rack on a rimmed baking sheet and place near the stove.

In a bowl, whisk together the flour, cornmeal, the remaining 2 teaspoons oregano, salt, and cayenne. Cut the calamari bodies crosswise into ¼-inch (6-mm) rings; leave the tentacles whole. Add one-third of the calamari to the flour mixture and toss to coat. Gently shake off the excess flour, then carefully add the calamari to the hot oil and deep-fry until golden brown, about 2 minutes. Using a wire skimmer or slotted spoon, transfer the fried calamari to the rack and keep warm while you coat and fry the remaining calamari in two batches.

Spoon the spicy marinara into individual dipping bowls. Transfer the fried calamari to a warmed platter and sprinkle with the parsley. Serve right away, passing the warm marinara sauce and the lemon wedges on the side.

FOR THE SPICY MARINARA

2 tablespoons olive oil

3 cloves garlic, minced

1½ cups (10½ oz/330 g) canned crushed plum tomatoes

1 teaspoon dried oregano

¼ teaspoon red pepper flakes

Canola oil for deep-frying

½ cup (2½ oz/75 g) all-purpose flour

½ cup (2½ oz/75 g) yellow cornmeal, preferably stone-ground

2 teaspoons dried oregano

1 teaspoon fine sea salt

¼ teaspoon cayenne pepper

1 lb (500 g) calamari, cleaned

Chopped fresh flat-leaf parsley for garnish

Lemon wedges for serving

If you really want to impress your friends at your next sports-inspired get-together, bake a batch of these guys. They are best enjoyed on the day you make them, ideally while they are still warm, as they don't keep well. This recipe offers four variations (see the following pages), so take full advantage of the dough to make two or three snacks on the same day.

SOFT PRETZELS WITH GRAINY MUSTARD MAKES 12 PRETZELS

FOR THE SOFT PRETZEL DOUGH

1 cup (250 ml) warm water (110°F/43°C)

1 package (2¼ teaspoons) active dry yeast

1 tablespoon sugar

3 tablespoons olive oil

3¼ cups (13 oz/390 g) all-purpose flour, plus more for dusting

1 teaspoon kosher salt

Vegetable oil for brushing

⅓ cup (2½ oz/75 g) baking soda

Coarse salt for sprinkling

Grainy mustard for serving

To make the dough, in the bowl of a stand mixer, stir together the warm water, yeast, and sugar. Let stand until foamy, about 10 minutes. Add the olive oil, flour, and kosher salt. Attach the dough hook and knead the dough on medium-low speed until smooth, about 10 minutes. Form the dough into a ball, cover the bowl with plastic wrap, and let rise in a warm spot until doubled in bulk, about 1 hour.

Line 2 baking sheets with parchment paper and brush the parchment with vegetable oil. Dump the dough onto a lightly floured work surface, then cut it into 12 equal pieces. Roll each piece into a rope about 18 inches (45 cm) long. With each rope positioned horizontally, bring the 2 ends up and toward the center as if forming an oval, cross one end over the other, and press each end into the bottom of the oval to create a pretzel shape. Place the pretzels on the prepared baking sheets, spacing them evenly.

Position a rack in the middle of the oven and preheat to 450°F (230°C). Fill a large, wide saucepan with 7 cups (1.75 l) water, stir in the baking soda, and bring to a boil over high heat. Gently drop 2 or 3 pretzels at a time into the boiling water (be careful not to overcrowd them). Boil for just under 1 minute, turning once with a large slotted spoon or spatula. Return the boiled pretzels to the baking sheets, top side up. Sprinkle with coarse salt and bake until golden brown, about 10 minutes, rotating the baking sheets about halfway through baking time. Serve warm with big spoonfuls of grainy mustard.

1 batch Soft Pretzel Dough (page 52)

6 tablespoons butter, melted

¾ cup (3 oz/90 g) freshly grated
Parmesan cheese

2 ½ tablespoons garlic salt

Freshly ground pepper

PARMESAN & GARLIC PRETZEL BITES MAKES 60 BITES

Make the pretzel dough. Prepare the boiling water, baking sheet, and oven as directed for the soft pretzels. Divide the dough into 12 equal pieces.

On a lightly floured work surface, roll each piece into a 1-by-6-inch (2.5-by-15-cm) stick and cut each stick crosswise into 5 pieces. Working in batches, gently lower the pretzel bites into the boiling water and cook for 1 minute.

Using a slotted spoon, transfer the bites to a mixing bowl and toss with the butter, Parmesan, and garlic salt. Transfer to the prepared baking sheet, season lightly with pepper, and bake until golden brown, 8–10 minutes. Serve right away.

1 batch Soft Pretzel Dough (page 52)

6 tablespoons butter, melted

½ cup (4 oz/125 g) sugar

1 tablespoon cinnamon

CINNAMON & SUGAR PRETZEL BITES MAKES 60 BITES

Make the pretzel dough. Prepare the boiling water, baking sheet, and oven as directed for the soft pretzels. Divide the dough into 12 equal pieces.

On a lightly floured work surface, roll each piece into a 1-by-6-inch (2.5-by-15-cm) stick and cut each stick crosswise into 5 pieces. Working in batches, gently lower the pretzel bites into the boiling water and cook for 1 minute.

Using a slotted spoon, transfer the bites to the prepared baking sheet and bake until golden brown, 8–10 minutes. Transfer to a mixing bowl and toss with the butter, sugar, and cinnamon. Serve right away.

PRETZEL STICKS WITH ALE CHEESE DIP MAKES 12 STICKS

1 batch Soft Pretzel Dough (page 52)

Coarse salt for sprinkling

FOR THE ALE CHEESE DIP

2 tablespoons butter

3 tablespoons all-purpose flour

¾ cup (180 ml) milk

¾ cup (180 ml) ale or dark beer

2 teaspoons Worcestershire sauce

1 teaspoon Dijon mustard

3 cups (12 oz/360 g) shredded sharp Cheddar cheese

Kosher salt and freshly ground pepper

Make the pretzel dough. Prepare the boiling water, baking sheet, and oven as directed for the soft pretzels. Divide the dough into 12 equal pieces.

On a lightly floured work surface, roll each piece into a 1-by-6-inch (2.5-by-15-cm) stick. Gently lower 2 or 3 pretzel sticks at a time into the boiling water. Boil for 1 minute, then transfer to the prepared baking sheet and season generously with coarse salt. Bake until golden brown, 10–12 minutes.

While the pretzel sticks are baking, prepare the cheese dip: In a saucepan over medium heat, melt the butter. Add the flour and cook, whisking constantly, for 1–2 minutes. Slowly whisk in the milk and beer and bring to a simmer. Add the Worcestershire sauce and mustard and cook, whisking constantly, until the mixture begins to thicken, about 2 minutes. Add the cheese, a handful at a time, stirring with a wooden spoon until melted. Season with salt and pepper and serve right away with the pretzel sticks for dipping.

PIGS IN A PRETZEL MAKES 40–42 PIECES

1 batch Soft Pretzel Dough (page 52)

14 hot dogs, each cut into 3 pieces, or 40 cocktail-size mini franks or sausages

Coarse salt for sprinkling

Mustard of choice for serving

Make the pretzel dough. Prepare the boiling water, baking sheets, and oven as directed for the soft pretzels. Cut the dough in half.

On a lightly floured work surface, roll one half of the dough into a 6-by-10-inch (15-by-25-cm) rectangle. Cut the dough crosswise into ten 1-inch (2.5-cm) strips, then halve them to 3 inches (7.5 cm) long.

Lay a piece of hot dog onto each piece of dough and wrap the dough around the hot dog, leaving the ends of the hot dog exposed. Pinch the ends firmly to seal. Repeat the process with the other half of the dough. Working in batches if necessary, gently lower the pigs into the boiling water and cook for 1 minute. Transfer to the prepared baking sheet and sprinkle with salt. Bake until golden brown, 10–12 minutes. Serve right away with mustard on the side for dipping.

Packed with bacon and three cheeses, coated with egg and bread crumbs, and deep-fried until golden and crisp, this sports bar staple is typically paired with cold beer to tamp down the heat. Seek out unblemished, bright green jalapeños for the best flavor.

JALAPEÑO POPPERS MAKES 12 POPPERS

In a frying pan over medium heat, fry the bacon, stirring occasionally, until crisp and browned, about 5 minutes. Transfer to paper towels to drain.

Using the tip of a paring knife, slit each chile on one side from the stem to the tip, leaving the stem end intact. Gently open up the chile and remove the seeds with the knife or a small spoon. Set aside.

In a small bowl, mix together the bacon, cream cheese, Cheddar, Monterey jack, and hot pepper sauce until well blended. Season to taste with salt and pepper. Using a small spoon, fill the chiles with the cheese mixture, dividing it evenly. Close the filled chiles, pressing firmly on the seams to close them.

In a small bowl, whisk together the eggs and milk. In a second shallow bowl, stir together the bread crumbs and a pinch each of salt and pepper. One at a time, dip the filled chiles into the egg mixture, allow the excess to drip off, then dip into the bread crumbs, patting gently to help them adhere. Transfer to a baking sheet. Let dry for about 10 minutes, then repeat to form a second coating, dipping the chiles first in the egg mixture and then in the crumbs.

Pour oil into a deep, heavy saucepan to a depth of at least 3 inches (7.5 cm). Over medium-high heat, warm the oil until it reaches 325°F (165°C) on a deep-fry thermometer. Preheat the oven to 200°F (95°C). Line a rimmed baking sheet with paper towels.

Working in batches to avoid crowding, carefully add the chiles to the hot oil and deep-fry, stirring occasionally with a wire skimmer, until golden brown, about 6 minutes. Using the skimmer, transfer to the prepared baking sheet and keep warm in the oven while you fry the remaining chiles. Serve the poppers hot.

2 thick-cut slices applewood-smoked bacon, finely chopped

12 small jalapeño chiles

4 oz (125 g) cream cheese, at room temperature

½ cup (2 oz/60 g) finely shredded sharp Cheddar cheese

½ cup (2 oz/60 g) finely shredded Monterey jack cheese

1 teaspoon hot pepper sauce, such as Tabasco

Kosher salt and freshly ground pepper

2 large eggs

1 tablespoon whole milk

1 cup (4 oz/125 g) fine dried bread crumbs or panko

Vegetable oil for deep-frying

Choose mushrooms that are firm, blemish-free, and a similar size to ensure they cook in the same amount of time. No matter which filling you decide to use, save what's left over and slip it into an omelet or a sandwich the next day.

STUFFED MUSHROOMS SERVES 4–6

1 tablespoon butter, at room temperature

24 large white or cremini mushrooms, stems removed and finely chopped, caps left whole

2 tablespoons olive oil

½ cup (2 oz/60 g) chopped yellow onion

Kosher salt and freshly ground pepper

Preheat the oven to 350°F (180°C). Coat the bottom of an 8-by-10-inch (20-by-25-cm) baking dish with butter. Place the mushroom caps, gill sides up, in a single layer in the baking dish and set aside.

In a frying pan over medium-high heat, warm the oil. Add the onion and chopped mushroom stems and season with salt and pepper. Sauté, stirring often, until soft, 6–8 minutes. Transfer to a mixing bowl and continue with one of the fillings below. Generously stuff the mushroom caps with the filling. Transfer to the oven and bake until the mushrooms are soft and the filling is warmed through, 25–30 minutes. Let cool slightly, then serve.

ITALIAN SAUSAGE Crumble 1 lb (500 g) Italian sausage meat into a frying pan. Cook over medium-high heat, breaking up the meat with a wooden spoon, until browned, about 8 minutes. Add to the onion mixture and let cool for 5 minutes. Stir in 8 oz (250 g) cream cheese, 2 tablespoons chopped fresh flat-leaf parsley, and ½ teaspoon garlic salt.

ARTICHOKE & GRUYÈRE To the onion mixture, add 1 can (14 oz/396 g) artichoke hearts, well drained and chopped; 3 green onions, chopped dark green parts only; 6 oz (185 g) shredded Gruyère cheese; and 4 oz (125 g) cream cheese. Season with salt and pepper.

SPINACH & PANCETTA Blanch one bunch of stemmed spinach leaves, drain, and squeeze dry to remove excess water. Chop and add to the onion mixture. In a frying pan over medium-high heat, cook 4 oz (125 g) pancetta, stirring often, until crispy, 8 minutes. Add the pancetta to the onion mixture along with 8 oz (250 g) cream cheese and 2 tablespoons grated pecorino cheese. Season with salt and pepper.

Slices of Italian sausage and tangles of sweet caramelized onion give this flatbread the appeal of pizza, yet it's much simpler to prepare. If the dough keeps springing back when you attempt to roll it out, let it rest for about 10 minutes, then try again. The dough is an easy canvas for a variety of toppings; double the dough recipe to make two variations at once.

CARAMELIZED ONION & SAUSAGE FLATBREAD SERVES 4–6

FOR THE FLATBREAD DOUGH

1¾ cups (7 oz/210 g) all-purpose flour, plus more for dusting

1 package (2¼ teaspoons) active dry yeast

1 teaspoon kosher salt

½ teaspoon sugar

¾ cup (180 ml) warm water (110°F/43°C)

Olive oil

FOR THE TOPPING

2 tablespoons olive oil, plus more for drizzling

2 large red onions

Kosher salt and freshly ground pepper

2 tablespoons balsamic vinegar

1 tablespoon fresh thyme leaves, chopped

3 links sweet or spicy Italian sausage

To make the dough, in a food processor, combine the flour, yeast, salt, and sugar, and pulse to mix. With the motor running, add the water in a steady stream and process until the dough comes together, about 20 seconds. Turn out onto a lightly floured work surface and knead until the dough is smooth and elastic, about 1 minute. Transfer to an oiled bowl and cover with a clean kitchen towel. Let the dough rise in a warm place until doubled in size, about 1 hour.

Meanwhile, make the topping: Peel the onions, cut in half lengthwise, then cut crosswise into slices. In a heavy frying pan over medium-high heat, warm the oil. Add the onions and cook, stirring often, until translucent, about 8 minutes. Reduce the heat to low, season to taste with salt and pepper, and sauté, stirring occasionally, until the onions turn deep brown, about 30 minutes. Stir in the vinegar and thyme and cook 3 minutes longer. Remove from the heat; set aside.

In a clean frying pan over medium-high heat, brown the sausages until cooked through, about 15 minutes. Transfer to a cutting board and cut into slices ¼-inch (6-mm) thick. Keep warm.

Punch down the dough and transfer to a lightly floured work surface. Cut into 4 equal pieces. Using a rolling pin, roll out each piece to a 10-inch (25-cm) round. Set a grill pan or cast-iron frying pan over high heat. Once the pan is extremely hot, working with one flatbread a time, lay the dough directly on the hot pan. Cook until bubbles appear, 1–2 minutes. Turn over and continue to cook until the bread is cooked through, about 2 more minutes.

Arrange the flatbreads on a platter. Top each with caramelized onions and sausage. Cut each flatbread into 6 pieces, finish with a drizzle of oil, and serve.

BRUSSELS SPROUTS, BACON & MOZZARELLA FLATBREAD SERVES 4

1 batch flatbread dough (page 60)

6 slices thick-cut bacon

¾ cup (2 oz/60 g) Brussels sprouts, halved and cored, outer leaves kept whole and the rest sliced

1 small red onion, thinly sliced

Kosher salt and freshly ground pepper

1½ teaspoons balsamic vinegar

8 oz (250 g) fresh mozzarella cheese, diced

Make the flatbread dough and let rise. Meanwhile, in a frying pan over medium-high heat, fry the bacon until crisp, about 6 minutes. Transfer to paper towels to drain. Cut into bite-size pieces. Set aside. Pour off all but 1 tablespoon of the grease from the pan and place over medium-high heat. Add the brussels sprouts and onion, season with salt and pepper, and sauté, stirring often, until softened and beginning to brown, about 5 minutes. Stir in the vinegar and sauté until the liquid is absorbed, about 2 minutes. Remove from the heat and set aside.

Punch down the dough and shape the flatbreads as directed. Cook as directed and, once you turn over each bread to cook the second side, sprinkle a quarter of the mozzarella over the top. When each bread is evenly charred and the cheese has melted, remove the bread from the heat and scatter a quarter of the brussels sprout mixture over the top. Cut each flatbread into 6 pieces and serve.

CORN, TOMATO & BASIL FLATBREAD SERVES 4

1 batch flatbread dough (page 60)

1 tablespoon olive oil

4 green onions, thinly sliced

¾ cup (4½ oz/140 g) corn kernels

1 cup (5 oz/140 g) cherry tomatoes, halved

1 teaspoon red wine vinegar

8 fresh basil leaves, sliced

1 cup (8 oz/250 g) basil pesto

½ cup (2 oz/60 g) crumbled feta cheese (optional)

Make the flatbread dough and let rise. Meanwhile, in a frying pan over medium-low heat, warm the oil. Add the onions and sauté, stirring often, until softened, about 3 minutes. Add the corn and cook, stirring, for 1 minute. Add the tomatoes and cook, stirring, until softened, about 1 minute. Add the vinegar and cook, stirring, for 30 seconds. Remove from the heat. Stir in the basil leaves.

Punch down the dough, shape the flatbreads, and cook as directed. Spread the pesto evenly over the cooked flatbreads. Scatter the tomato-corn mixture over the pesto and sprinkle with feta cheese, if desired. Cut each flatbread into 6 pieces and serve.

SET THE STAGE

A serving board of rustic slate or reclaimed wood is a graceful yet casual way to serve this favorite—scatter the wedges with fresh green herbs for a bright final touch.

Corn, Tomato
& Basil Flatbread
Page 61

Caramelized Onion
& Sausage Flatbread
Page 60

Whether you pile flatbread high with perfect summer tomatoes in August or hearty sausage and onions on a winter evening, it's a versatile choice for easy entertaining.

FLATBREAD FOR A CROWD

Brussels Sprouts, Bacon & Mozzarella Flatbread
Page 61

When a hungry hoard comes to watch the game, this super-sized sandwich is your go-to solution. To make snacktime easy, place the whole sub on a long cutting board with a good serrated bread knife and a stack of plates alongside for DIY service. If it is a vegetarian crowd, use mozzarella, roasted red peppers, and olives in place of the cured meats.

ITALIAN SUB SERVES 6

To make the aioli, combine the garlic and a big pinch of salt in a food processor. Pulse several times until the garlic is finely chopped. Add the egg and egg yolk and pulse to combine. With the motor running, slowly drip a few drops of oil, then follow with a slow and steady stream of oil. Continue to purée until fully combined. Transfer to a bowl, stir in the lemon zest and juice, and season with additional salt, if needed. Set aside.

Lay the baguette, cut sides open, on a large cutting board. Slather the aioli onto both sides of the bread. Over the bottom half of the baguette, layer the cheese and meats, followed by the lettuce, tomatoes, peperoncini, and red pepper. Cover with the top half, cut into 2½-inch (6-cm) pieces, and serve.

FOR THE LEMON AIOLI

1 clove garlic

Kosher salt

1 large egg plus 1 large egg yolk

1 cup (250 ml) canola or vegetable oil

Zest and juice of 1 lemon

1 Italian baguette, halved horizontally

6 slices provolone cheese

½ lb (250 g) thinly sliced ham

½ lb (250 g) thinly sliced salami

⅓ lb (150 g) thinly sliced coppa or soppressata

1 cup (1 oz/30 g) shredded lettuce

2 Roma tomatoes, sliced

⅓ cup (2½ oz/70 g) sliced peperoncini

1 red bell pepper, roasted, seeded, and sliced

Fragrant coriander, turmeric, cumin, and saffron and pungent fresh ginger and garlic infuse this yogurt-based marinade with outsized Indian flavor. Don't be tempted to use chicken breasts here, as thighs stand up better to the bold spice mixture and remain more succulent over the hot fire.

TANDOORI CHICKEN KEBABS SERVES 6

FOR THE MARINADE

2 cups (16 oz/500 g) plain whole-milk yogurt

2 tablespoons fresh lemon juice

2 tablespoons peeled and minced fresh ginger

4 cloves garlic, minced

1 teaspoon *each* ground coriander and ground turmeric

½ teaspoon *each* saffron threads, ground cumin, and cayenne pepper

Kosher salt and freshly ground pepper

8 boneless, skinless chicken thighs (3 lb/1.5 kg)

6–12 metal or wooden skewers

1 small red onion, thinly sliced and separated into rings

¼ cup (⅓ oz/10 g) chopped fresh cilantro

Lemon wedges for serving

To make the marinade, in a bowl, whisk together the yogurt, lemon juice, ginger, garlic, coriander, turmeric, saffron, cumin, cayenne, 1 teaspoon salt, and ½ teaspoon black pepper.

Cut the chicken thighs into 1-inch (2.5-cm) cubes. Place the chicken cubes in a large lock-top plastic bag and pour in the marinade. Seal the bag closed, massage the marinade around the chicken, and refrigerate overnight.

At least 30 minutes before grilling, remove the chicken from the refrigerator. Discard the marinade. If using wooden skewers, soak them in water for 30 minutes.

Prepare a charcoal or gas grill for direct grilling over high heat. Brush and oil the grill grate.

Thread the chicken cubes onto the skewers without crowding them. Place the skewers on the grill directly over the fire and cook, turning once, until the chicken is lightly grill-marked on both sides and opaque throughout but still moist, about 5 minutes per side. If the chicken begins to burn, move the skewers to the edge of a charcoal grill or lower the heat of a gas grill.

Slide the chicken off the skewers onto a platter. Top with the onion and cilantro and serve with lemon wedges.

If the weather is too cold for outdoor grilling, these wings can be cooked in the oven with similarly delicious results. Place the spice-rubbed wings on a foil-lined rimmed baking sheet and bake in a preheated 400°F (200°C) oven, turning once, until cooked through, about 45 minutes, then coat them with the sauce as directed for the grilled wings.

SPICY BUFFALO WINGS SERVES 6–8

3 lb (1.5 kg) chicken wings, tips removed

3 tablespoons canola oil

2 tablespoons All-Purpose BBQ Rub (page 100)

½ cup (4 oz/125 g) unsalted butter

6 cloves garlic, minced

½ cup (125 ml) hot pepper sauce, such as Tabasco

1 tablespoon distilled white vinegar

Blue Cheese Dip (page 100) for serving

Celery sticks for serving

In a large bowl, combine the wings and oil. Toss until the wings are evenly coated. Sprinkle the BBQ rub over the wings and toss again to coat evenly. Cover and refrigerate overnight.

At least 30 minutes before grilling, remove the wings from the refrigerator. In a large frying pan over medium heat, melt the butter. Add the garlic and cook, stirring, until fragrant and tender, about 2 minutes. Pour in the hot sauce and vinegar, stir well, remove from the heat, and set the pan aside.

Prepare a charcoal or gas grill for direct grilling over high heat. Brush and oil the grill grate.

Place the chicken wings on the grill directly over the fire and cook, turning frequently, until they are nicely browned on all sides, have some char, and are tender, 15–20 minutes.

Transfer the wings to the sauce in the frying pan, place the pan over low heat, and toss the wings in the sauce to coat evenly. Let the wings and the sauce marry for about 5 minutes.

Transfer the wings to a platter and pour any remaining pan sauce over the top. Serve with the blue cheese dip and celery sticks.

SWEET JALAPEÑO WINGS SERVES 4

3 lb (1.5 kg) chicken wings, tips removed

¼ cup (60 ml) canola oil

Kosher salt and ground pepper

4 tablespoons (2 oz/60 g) unsalted butter

¼ cup (2 ½ oz/75 g) jalapeño jelly or pepper jelly

2 tablespoons honey or light agave syrup

2 jalapeño chiles, seeded and finely chopped

1 teaspoon granulated garlic

½ teaspoon *each* paprika, chile powder, and cayenne pepper

In a large bowl, combine the wings and oil, toss to coat, and season with salt and black pepper. Cook as directed on facing page.

In a small saucepan over medium heat, melt the butter. Stir in the jalapeño jelly, honey, chiles, garlic, paprika, chile powder, cayenne, and a pinch each of salt and pepper. Keep warm.

In a large bowl, combine the cooked chicken wings and the jalapeño mixture and toss to coat. Transfer to a serving plate and serve at once.

HONEY-SESAME WINGS SERVES 4

3 lb (1.5 kg) chicken wings, tips removed

¼ cup (60 ml) canola oil

2 tablespoons shichimi togarashi spice blend or lemon pepper

¾ cup (180 ml) sweet hot chile sauce

¼ cup (60 ml) teriyaki sauce

2 tablespoons *each* Asian sesame oil and honey

Juice of 1 lime

2 tablespoons toasted sesame seeds or thinly sliced green onions, optional

In a large bowl, combine the wings and oil and toss until the wings are evenly coated. Sprinkle the shichimi togarashi over the wings and toss to coat evenly. Set aside at room temperature for about 30 minutes.

In a small saucepan, stir together the chile sauce, teriyaki sauce, sesame oil, and honey. Place over low heat and , stirring, bring to a gentle simmer. Remove from the heat and let cool slightly. Stir in the lime juice. Set aside.

Cook the wings as directed on the facing page. Transfer the cooked wings to a large bowl, pour the glaze over them, and toss to coat evenly. Let sit for about 5 minutes to allow the flavors to meld, then transfer to a platter, sprinkle with the sesame seeds or green onions, if using, and serve at once.

SWEET & SPICY WINGS

*Spicy Buffalo Wings
Page 68*

NAPKINS REQUIRED

When serving game-day favorites like buffalo wings, don't neglect the extras—set out plenty of flavorful creamy dip, icy cold beer, and a stack of large napkins.

*Blue Cheese Dip
Page 100*

ADD SOME HEAT

Bar food isn't the same without hot sauce on the side, so be sure to have Sriracha or freshly sliced jalapeños on hand for guests who crave spicy flavors.

Sweet Jalapeño Wings
Page 69

Honey-Sesame Wings
Page 69

A few sophisticated additions are all you need to turn everyday quesadillas into party fare, especially if you cook up two or three of the variations here. Best of all, you can assemble the quesadillas a few hours ahead, refrigerate them, and then cook them as needed. If the weather is good, and the grill is already going, move the cooking outdoors.

BARBECUED CHICKEN & AVOCADO QUESADILLAS SERVES 4

Place the chicken breast in a saucepan and cover it with 1 inch (2.5 cm) cold water. Bring to a boil over medium-high heat, reduce the heat to low, and simmer until the chicken is opaque throughout, about 20 minutes. Drain, then shred and transfer to a mixing bowl. Stir in the barbecue sauce.

Lay two tortillas on a work surface and cover with the cheese, chicken, and avocado. Sprinkle with salt and pepper. Top with the remaining tortillas. Heat a large frying pan over medium-high heat and add half the butter. Use the other half of the butter to coat the tops of the quesadillas. Carefully transfer the quesadillas to the pan. Cook until golden brown, about 3 minutes. Carefully flip and continue to cook until the cheese is melted and the tortilla is golden brown, about 3 minutes longer. Transfer to a cutting board, cut each into 8 wedges, and serve.

GREEK Fill the tortillas with 6 cups (6 oz/180 g) blanched and squeezed-dry fresh spinach, 2 chopped Roma tomatoes, 1/3 cup (2 oz/50 g) pitted and sliced kalamata olives, 1 cup (4 oz/125 g) shredded mozzarella cheese, and 1/2 cup (2 oz/60 g) crumbled feta cheese.

SHRIMP & POBLANO PEPPER Toss 1/2 lb (250 g) shelled and deveined medium shrimp with 2 teaspoons olive oil, 2 teaspoons chili powder, and 1 teaspoon salt. Add to a very hot frying pan over high heat and sauté, turning once, until cooked through, about 5 minutes total. Cut the shrimp in half horizontally. Roast, peel, seed, and chop 1 large poblano chile. Fill tortillas with 1 1/2 cups (6 oz/180 g) shredded Monterey jack cheese, the shrimp, and chiles. Serve with salsa, if desired.

1 boneless, skinless chicken breast (about 1/2 lb/250 g)

6 tablespoons (3 oz/90 g) Classic BBQ Sauce (page 100) or store-bought sauce

4 (8-inch/20-cm) flour or corn tortillas

1 1/2 cups (6 oz/190 g) shredded mozzarella cheese

1 ripe avocado, sliced

Kosher salt and freshly ground pepper

1 tablespoon butter, at room temperature

Roasted Tomato Salsa (page 21) or store-bought salsa for serving (optional)

Whether you are gathered around the TV or the tailgate, a plate of deviled eggs is a welcome sight. If you can't find fresh tarragon, use fresh chervil or even fennel fronds in its place. To give the filling a more devilish profile, add a dash or two of Sriracha or other hot pepper sauce, then finish with a sprinkling of paprika or ground cayenne pepper.

CLASSIC DEVILED EGGS SERVES 6–12

6 large eggs, at room temperature

2 tablespoons mayonnaise

2 teaspoons Dijon mustard

1 teaspoon white wine vinegar

1 tablespoon drained and chopped capers or cornichon pickles, plus whole capers or chopped cornichons for garnish

1 tablespoon chopped fresh chives, plus more for garnish

1½ teaspoons chopped fresh tarragon

Kosher salt and freshly ground pepper

Gently place the eggs in a saucepan and add tepid water to cover by about 2 inches (5 cm). Bring to a boil over high heat, then reduce the heat to low and simmer, uncovered, for 10 minutes. Using a slotted spoon, transfer the eggs to a colander and place under cold running water until cool.

Carefully peel the eggs and cut in half lengthwise. Remove the yolks and put them in a small bowl. Place the whites, cavity side up, on a clean work surface or plate.

Add the mayonnaise, mustard, and vinegar to the bowl with the yolks. Using a fork, mash and mix to form a paste. Stir in the capers, chives, and tarragon. Season with salt and pepper. Spoon the yolk mixture back into the cavities of the egg whites, dividing it evenly and mounding it in the center. Alternatively, spoon the yolk mixture into a pastry bag fitted with a large plain or star tip and pipe the mixture into the whites.

Arrange the deviled eggs on a platter. Garnish with chives and more salt and pepper, dot with whole capers, and serve right away.

PACK TO GO I like to bring deviled eggs to a party or picnic—they are crowd-pleasers and easy to prepare—but I don't find them appealing if they've been assembled too far in advance. Here's my easy-to-transport solution: Hard-cook the eggs and make the filling ahead, then store the whites and filling in two separate zip-lock plastic bags. When I arrive at a party, I snip off the corner of the plastic bag holding the filling and pipe it into the whites.

Romesco sauce—a punchier Spanish version of tomato sauce full of garlic, roasted peppers, and ground almonds—is a tasty partner to classic meatballs. Romesco is traditionally served at room temperature, but can be warmed as a toasty accompaniment to hot meatballs, or both can be served at room temperature.

MEATBALLS WITH ROMESCO SAUCE SERVES 4–6

Make the romesco sauce; set aside.

To make the meatballs, in a small bowl, soak the bread in the milk for 10 minutes, turning to moisten it evenly. Squeeze most of the milk from the bread and tear the bread into small pieces. In a large bowl, combine the bread, pork, beef, onion, parsley, oregano, Parmesan, egg, ½ teaspoon salt, and a good grinding of pepper. Blend with a fork, breaking up the ground meat, and then, with clean hands, mix thoroughly. Chill for 1 hour.

Line a rimmed baking sheet with parchment paper. Use an ice-cream scoop to form about 18 meatballs the size of golf balls, placing them on the prepared baking sheet. Chill again for 1 hour.

Preheat the broiler and place a rack about 3 inches (7.5 cm) from the heat source. Slide the baking sheet under the broiler and brown the meatballs, turning them once or twice with tongs, until golden brown and firm, 8–15 minutes. To test the meatballs, cut into one to make sure it is no longer pink at the center.

Serve the romesco sauce warm or at room temperature. To serve it warm, place the sauce in a bowl set over gently simmering water in a pan and cover, stirring occasionally, until warm, 3–4 minutes.

Serve the meatballs alongside the sauce for dipping, or transfer the meatballs to the warm sauce, cover, and cook for 5 minutes, turning the meatballs occasionally and spooning the sauce over the top. Serve right away.

Romesco sauce (page 101)

FOR THE MEATBALLS

6 slices sandwich-style white bread, crusts removed

¾ cup (180 ml) whole milk

½ lb (250 g) ground pork

¼ lb (125 g) ground beef chuck (20 percent fat)

1 small white or yellow onion, finely chopped

¼ cup (⅓ oz/10 g) minced fresh flat-leaf parsley and/or dill

1 tablespoon dried oregano

¼ cup (1 oz/30 g) freshly grated Parmesan cheese

1 large egg, lightly beaten

Kosher salt and freshly ground pepper

Homemade tortilla bowls are a snap to prepare and provide a crisp base for a colorful array of savory ingredients. Be generous when adding the cilantro dressing, as it adds a bright, piquant taste to the flavor-packed salad. You can substitute any other protein, such as skirt steak or shrimp, for the chicken.

CHICKEN TACO SALAD IN CRISPY TORTILLA BOWLS SERVES 4

4 (8-inch/20-cm) flour tortillas

3 tablespoons olive oil

3 boneless, skinless chicken thighs (about 1¼ lb/625 g total weight)

1½ teaspoons chili powder

Kosher salt and freshly ground pepper

Creamy Cilantro Dressing (page 101)

1 head romaine lettuce, chopped

½ can (7½ oz/235 g) black beans, drained and rinsed

¾ cup (about 4 oz/125 g) cherry tomatoes, halved

1 ripe avocado, cubed

½ cup (2 oz/60 g) shredded Cheddar cheese

¼ cup (1 oz/30 g) diced red onion, optional

½ cup (4 oz/125 g) Roasted Tomato Salsa (page 21) or store-bought salsa

Preheat the oven to 375°F (190°C).

Brush both sides of the tortillas with 2 tablespoons of the oil. Turn a 12-cup muffin pan upside down and nestle the tortillas between the cups to make four lopsided bowls. (They don't have to be perfect.) Bake until golden brown and crispy, 10–12 minutes. Let them cool on the muffin pan and set aside.

Brush the chicken with the remaining 1 tablespoon oil and season with chili powder, salt, and pepper. Transfer to a baking sheet and bake until cooked through, about 22 minutes. Keep warm.

To assemble, toss the lettuce with cilantro dressing and divide among the 4 taco bowls. Top each with beans, tomatoes, avocado, cheese, and red onion, if using. Cut the chicken into bite-size pieces and add to the bowls. Finish with a generous dollop of salsa and serve.

A cousin to both the pizza and the calzone, a stromboli is basically a rolled pizza. It is easy to cut into slices and can be prepared a day ahead and gently reheated or served at room temperature—two sure-fire selling points for any cook who is planning a party menu.

HAM, CHEESE & SUN-DRIED TOMATO STROMBOLI SERVES 4

1 ball Stromboli Dough (page 101) or 1 round store-bought pizza dough

1½ tablespoons olive oil

1 cup (4 oz/125 g) shredded sharp Cheddar cheese

3 oz (90 g) sliced ham, chopped

¼ cup (2 oz/60 g) sun-dried tomatoes in oil, drained

¼ cup (¼ oz/8 g) fresh basil leaves

Kosher salt and freshly ground pepper

1 large egg, beaten with 1 tablespoon water

Make the stromboli dough. Cover with a clean kitchen towel and set aside.

Place a pizza stone in the oven and preheat to 450°F (230°C), letting the pizza stone heat for an additional 15–30 minutes without opening the oven door.

Roll out the dough to a 10-by-14-inch (25-by-35-cm) rectangle. Brush the dough with the oil and scatter the cheese over the top, leaving a 1-inch (2.5 cm) border on the short sides and a 3-inch (7.5-cm) border on the long side farthest away from you. Top the cheese with the ham, sun-dried tomatoes, and basil. Season with salt and pepper.

Fold the two uncovered short sides over the filling. Keeping the short sides folded, and beginning on the long end closest to you, tightly roll up the stromboli and pinch the edge to the side of the roll to seal it. Place the roll, seam side down, on a well-floured pizza peel. Brush the outside of the stromboli with the egg wash and, using the tip of a sharp knife, make a few slits every 2 inches (5 cm) down the length of the roll. Season with salt and pepper. Carefully transfer the stromboli to the pizza stone in the oven, keeping it seam side down. Bake until golden brown, 15–18 minutes. Transfer to a cutting board and let rest for 5 minutes before carefully slicing and serving.

Stuffed potato skins are satisfying, easy to prepare, and can be filled with countless savory mixtures. Load the skins with this mix of creamy goat cheese and caramelized onions, or swap out the filling for any of the variations offered below.

POTATO SKINS WITH CARAMELIZED ONIONS & CHEESE SERVES 8

Preheat the oven to 450°F (230°C). Prick the potatoes all over with a fork, and place on a baking sheet. Bake until fork-tender, about 1 hour. Remove and let cool slightly, then cut in half lengthwise and remove the flesh, leaving ¼ inch (6 mm) around the perimeter. Reserve the potato flesh for another use.

Preheat the broiler. Place the potato skins in a single layer on a baking sheet and brush both sides with butter. Broil 4 minutes, turn over, and continue to broil until the edges are golden brown, about 4 minutes longer.

To make the filling, in a frying pan over high heat, warm the oil and butter. Add the onions, season with salt and pepper, and sauté, stirring often, until softened, about 8 minutes. Reduce the heat to low and continue to cook, stirring occasionally, until deep brown, about 20 minutes. Stir in the vinegar and thyme and cook for 10 minutes. Spoon the onions into the potato skins, then divide the goat cheese over the top. Return the filled skins to the broiler and cook just until the cheese is melted, about 4 minutes. Transfer to a platter and serve.

PANCETTA & CHEDDAR In a frying pan over medium heat, fry 10 oz (315 g) diced pancetta until crispy. Divide the pancetta, 3 chopped green onions, and 2 cups (8 oz/250 g) shredded Cheddar cheese among the skins.

TOMATO, CHIVES & GRUYÈRE Divide 6 diced Roma tomatoes, ¼ cup (⅓ oz/10 g) chopped fresh chives, and 2 cups (8 oz/250 g) shredded Gruyère cheese among the skins.

REUBEN Divide ¼ lb (125 g) sliced corned beef, 2 cups (16 oz/1 kg) sauerkraut, 1 cup (8 oz/250 g) Thousand Island dressing, and 8 halved slices Swiss cheese among the skins.

8 russet potatoes (about 3 lb/1.5 kg total weight), scrubbed and patted dry

4 tablespoons (2 oz/60 g) butter, melted

FOR THE ONION & CHEESE FILLING

2 tablespoons olive oil

2 tablespoons butter

4 yellow onions, halved and thinly sliced

Kosher salt and freshly ground pepper

2 tablespoons balsamic vinegar

1 tablespoon chopped fresh thyme

6 oz (190 g) crumbled goat cheese

FULLY LOADED POTATO SKINS

Caramelized Onion & Cheese Potato Skin

HELP YOURSELF

Set up a fan-friendly baked potato bar by setting out all the ingredients before your guests arrive. Find these variations on page 79.

Pancetta & Cheddar Potato Skin

Tomato, Chives & Gruyère Potato Skin

A PERFECT PLATFORM

Russet potatoes make an appetizing canvas for a huge variety of toppings that range from sophisticated to sublimely simple.

Reuben Potato Skin

In the Carolinas, "real" barbecue is languidly cooked in a smoker with hickory wood, but more people likely make it this way in the oven. It takes awhile, but what a payoff: soft rolls piled high with barbecue sauce–slathered pork and homey coleslaw. See image on page 84.

PULLED PORK SLIDERS MAKES 10 SLIDERS

1 bone-in pork shoulder
(about 7½ lb/3.75 kg)

2 teaspoons sweet paprika, preferably Hungarian or Spanish

¾ teaspoon dried thyme

¾ teaspoon dried oregano

Kosher salt and freshly ground black pepper

⅛ teaspoon cayenne pepper

2½ cups (625 ml) cider vinegar

1 yellow onion, chopped

5 cloves garlic, minced

¼ cup (2 oz/60 g) lightly packed golden brown sugar

¼ cup (60 g) Homemade Ketchup (page 100) or store-bought ketchup

1 teaspoon red pepper flakes

⅓ cup (80 ml) canola oil

1 small head red or green cabbage, cored and shredded

10 soft slider buns, split

Place a rack in the lower third of the oven and preheat to 325°F (165°C). Cut the rind off the pork shoulder, leaving a thin layer of fat. Using a sharp knife, score the fat in a crosshatch pattern, creating 1-inch (2.5-cm) diamonds. In a small bowl, mix the paprika, thyme, oregano, 2 teaspoons salt, ½ teaspoon black pepper, and the cayenne. Sprinkle the mixture evenly over the pork and rub it in. Place the pork in a large Dutch oven and add ½ cup (125 ml) of the vinegar, the onion, and two-thirds of the garlic. Cover and bake, turning the pork every hour or so, until it is fork-tender and an instant-read thermometer inserted in the thickest part away from the bone registers at least 190°F (90°C), 5–6 hours.

Meanwhile, in a bowl, whisk together the remaining 2 cups (500 ml) vinegar, the remaining garlic, the brown sugar, ketchup, and pepper flakes. The sauce will be thin. Measure out ¼ cup (60 ml) sauce, then transfer the remaining sauce to a covered container and set aside at room temperature. In a bowl, whisk together the ¼ cup (60 ml) barbecue sauce and the oil. Add the cabbage and mix to coat evenly. Season with salt and pepper. Cover and refrigerate for at least 2 hours to allow the cabbage to soften and the flavors to blend.

When the pork is ready, transfer it to a carving board and tent with aluminum foil. Let rest for at least 20 minutes. Meanwhile, skim the fat from the cooking liquid, then boil the liquid over high heat until reduced to about ¾ cup (180 ml). Using 2 forks, pull the pork shoulder into shreds. (Once the pork has been pulled apart into large chunks, it may be easier to use a knife to help shred the meat.) Transfer to a serving bowl and moisten with the reduced cooking liquid. To serve, heap the pulled pork and a spoonful of the slaw onto the bottom half of each bun and cover with the bun top. Serve, passing the sauce on the side.

Once known as the butcher's tenderloin, hanger steak has a deep, rich flavor that holds its own alongside tart blue cheese and sweet onions. Layering this trio of ingredients on soft buns results in delicious sliders that will satisfy any crowd.

HANGER STEAK SLIDERS MAKES 12 SLIDERS

To make the marinade, in a small bowl, combine the tamari, olive oil, vinegar, garlic, mustards, mustard seeds, ginger, a pinch of salt, and 1 teaspoon pepper. You should have about ¾ cup (180 ml) marinade. Place the hanger steaks in a large lock-top plastic bag and pour in the marinade. Seal the bag closed, massage the marinade around the meat, and refrigerate overnight.

At least 30 minutes before grilling, remove the steaks from the refrigerator. Discard the marinade and pat the steaks dry with paper towels. Brush the steaks with canola oil.

Prepare a charcoal or gas grill for direct grilling over high heat. Brush and oil the grill grate.

In a sauté pan over low heat, melt the butter. Add the onions and cook slowly, stirring often, until they are tender and caramelized, about 20 minutes. Remove from the heat and keep warm. (If necessary, reheat just before serving.)

Place the steaks on the grill directly over the fire and cook, turning once, until nicely charred on both sides and barely firm to the touch, about 4 minutes per side for medium-rare or 6 minutes per side for medium. Transfer the steaks to a carving board and let rest for about 5 minutes. Meanwhile, put the buns, cut sides down, on the edge of the grill to toast for about 1 minute.

Thinly slice the steaks against the grain, capturing any released juices. Toss the sliced meat and juices together in a bowl. Divide the meat and juices evenly among the bun bottoms. Top with the cheese and then with the onions, dividing them both evenly. Cap with the bun tops and serve right away.

FOR THE BALSAMIC-MUSTARD MARINADE

¼ cup (60 ml) tamari or reduced-sodium soy sauce

¼ cup (60 ml) extra-virgin olive oil

¼ cup (60 ml) balsamic vinegar

6 cloves garlic, finely minced or pressed

2 tablespoons whole-grain mustard

1 tablespoon Dijon mustard

1 tablespoon yellow or brown mustard seeds

2 teaspoons peeled and grated fresh ginger

Kosher salt and freshly ground pepper

4 hanger steaks, each about 6 oz (185 g)

Canola oil for brushing

1 tablespoon unsalted butter

2 sweet onions, thinly sliced

12 slider buns or sourdough rolls, split

¼ lb (125 g) blue cheese, crumbled

Inspired by the famed green chile cheeseburgers of New Mexico, this adaptation uses ground buffalo instead of the traditional beef and spikes the mayonnaise with lime juice and chipotle chile. You can shape the burgers and refrigerate them up to several hours in advance so they are ready for the grill when it's time to cook.

SOUTHWESTERN BUFFALO BURGER SLIDERS MAKES 6 SLIDERS

To make the chipotle mayo, in a bowl, stir together the mayonnaise, chipotle chile, cilantro, and lime juice. Season with salt and pepper. Use right away, or store in an airtight container in the refrigerator for up to 1 week.

Prepare a charcoal or gas grill for direct grilling over high heat. Brush and oil the grill grate.

Divide the meat into 6 equal portions. Shape each portion into a patty about 1 inch (2.5 cm) thick, being careful not to compact the meat too much. Season on both sides with salt and pepper. Make a depression in the center of each patty with your thumb. Refrigerate the patties until the grill is ready.

Place the patties, indented side up, on the grill directly over the fire and cook until nicely charred on both sides, about 5 minutes per side. During the last 2 minutes of cooking, divide the green chiles evenly among the patties, arranging them on top, and then top each patty with a slice of cheese. Place the rolls, cut side down, along the edge of the grill and cover the grill. Grill until the cheese is melted and the rolls are lightly toasted.

Place the burgers on the roll bottoms and place the tops alongside. Serve with the chipotle mayo and the tomato slices, if using.

FOR THE CHIPOTLE MAYO

1 cup (250 ml) mayonnaise

1 chipotle chile in adobo sauce, chopped

2 tablespoons chopped fresh cilantro

Juice from ¼ lime

Kosher salt and freshly ground pepper

2 lb (1 kg) ground buffalo

Kosher salt and freshly ground pepper

½ cup (4 oz/125 g) chopped roasted green chiles, jarred or thawed frozen

6 slices Monterey jack cheese

6 slider rolls, split

6 thick tomato slices (optional)

These unfussy—and utterly satisfying—sandwiches are a perfect match for a sports-inspired gathering. The savory ground-beef filling gets extra flavor from a delicious combination of spices and ingredients. Double the recipe to feed a crowd.

SLOPPY JOES SERVES 4

1 tablespoon olive oil, if needed

1¼ lb (625 g) ground beef or ground turkey

2 tablespoons firmly packed golden brown sugar

2 tablespoons dried minced onion

1 teaspoon paprika

1 teaspoon chili powder

½ teaspoon garlic powder

1 can (15 oz/425 g) tomato sauce

2 tablespoons tomato paste

2 tablespoons Worcestershire sauce

2 teaspoons red wine vinegar

Kosher salt and freshly ground pepper

4 hamburger buns or brioche rolls, split

Place a large frying pan over medium-high heat. If you are using turkey, add the oil to the skillet to keep it from sticking. Add the meat and cook, using a wooden spoon to break it up into small pieces, until evenly cooked, 8–10 minutes. Reduce the heat to medium-low and add the brown sugar, onion, paprika, chili powder, and garlic powder. Cook, stirring, until blended, about 2 minutes.

Add the tomato sauce, tomato paste, Worcestershire sauce, and vinegar. Stir until well mixed. Bring to a boil over high heat. Immediately reduce the heat to medium-low and cook, stirring often to blend the flavors, about 5 minutes longer. Season with salt and pepper.

Place a bun bottom, cut side up, on each of 4 plates. Spoon an equal amount of the meat mixture over the buns, then cover with the bun tops. Serve hot.

This restaurant classic is infused with a sultry blend of flavors. The ribs spend hardly any time on the grill, but they should marinate overnight. The salty, sweet, hot, tangy marinade and sweet-hot sauce also pair well with chicken and pork.

KOREAN SHORT RIBS SERVES 6

To make the marinade, in a large bowl, combine the soy sauce, brown sugar, vinegar, sesame oil, garlic, ginger, ketchup, and pepper flakes and whisk to dissolve the sugar.

Place the ribs in a large lock-top plastic bag and pour in the marinade. Seal the bag closed, massage the marinade around the ribs, and refrigerate overnight. Be sure to turn the bag over several times while the ribs are marinating.

To make the barbecue sauce, in a bowl, whisk together the hoisin sauce, pepper sauce, mirin, sesame oil, and ¼ cup (60 ml) water. Taste and adjust the seasoning with more sesame oil, if desired. You should have about 1 cup (250 ml). Use right away, or store in an airtight container in the refrigerator for up to 2 months. Bring to room temperature before using.

Prepare a charcoal or gas grill for direct grilling over high heat. Brush and oil the grill grate.

Remove the ribs from the marinade and discard the marinade. Pat the ribs dry with paper towels. Place the ribs on the grill directly over the fire and cook, turning once, until medium, 6–8 minutes total. During the last 2 minutes of cooking, brush the ribs with some of the barbecue sauce. Transfer the ribs to a platter and let rest for 5–10 minutes. Serve with the remaining barbecue sauce on the side.

FOR THE SOY MARINADE

½ cup (125 ml) reduced-sodium soy sauce

¼ cup (2 oz/60 g) firmly packed golden brown sugar

2 tablespoons rice vinegar

2 tablespoons Asian sesame oil

2 tablespoons minced garlic

1 tablespoon peeled and finely chopped fresh ginger

1 tablespoon ketchup

1 teaspoon red pepper flakes

5 lb (2.5 kg) flanken-cut beef short ribs, prepared by your butcher

FOR THE ASIAN-STYLE BARBECUE SAUCE

¼ cup (60 ml) hoisin sauce

¼ cup (60 ml) sweet-hot pepper sauce

2 tablespoons mirin

1 tablespoon Asian sesame oil

Most die-hard sports fans consider sweet-hot baby back ribs de rigueur at any game-day get-together. Hickory, oak, or maple wood chips are a good choice with pork, or you can opt for a sweeter fruit wood, such as cherry or peach. Be sure to set out a big stack of napkins alongside the platter of ribs.

BARBECUED BABY BACK RIBS SERVES 4

2 racks baby back ribs,
about 3 lb (1.5 kg) each

2–3 tablespoons mustard of choice

All-Purpose BBQ Rub (page 100)

2 cups (500 g) Classic BBQ Sauce
(page 100) or store-bought barbecue
sauce

2 tablespoons honey

Preheat the oven to 250°F (120°C). Remove the membrane from the back of each rack and trim off any excess fat. Brush with the mustard and sprinkle the rub on both sides of the racks. Gently pat the rub into the mustard. Place the ribs, side by side, on a large piece of aluminum foil and loosely wrap the ribs. Set on a rimmed baking sheet. Unwrap one corner and pour in ¼ cup (60 ml) water; reseal the package. Bake the ribs for 1 hour.

Prepare a charcoal or gas grill for indirect grilling over medium-low heat; the temperature of the grill should be 300°–350°F (150°–180°C). If using charcoal, bank the lit coals on either side of the grill bed, leaving a strip in the center without heat. Place a drip pan in the center and fill with water. If using gas, turn off one or more burners to create a cooler zone. Brush and oil the grill grate.

Remove the ribs from the oven. Unwrap the ribs and discard the foil. Place the ribs, meat sides down, on the grill over the indirect-heat area, cover the grill, and cook for 1 hour.

If using a charcoal grill, light some coals in a charcoal chimney to raise the temperature of the fire to medium (about 375°F/190°C). Uncover the grill and add the hot coals. If using a gas grill, uncover the grill and raise the heat to medium. Move the ribs, meat side down, to the direct-heat area of the grill and brush with the BBQ sauce. Cook for 5 minutes, then turn the ribs and brush the bone sides with sauce. Continue to cook for 20 minutes, turning and basting with sauce every 5 minutes. On the last turn, drizzle the honey on the meaty side of the racks.

Transfer the racks to a carving board and let rest for 10 minutes. Cut the racks into individual ribs, pile them on a platter, and serve with the remaining sauce.

Bloody Mary

DRINKS
FOR A
CROWD

Greyhound

POUR FROM PITCHERS

Refreshing cocktails mixed ahead
of time and served from pitchers
make it easy to get a cold drink into
the hands of your guests quickly.

Ginger Shandy

Mint Mojito

MIX IN FRESH HERBS

For small casual gatherings, keep bar options simple and serve beer, chilled white wine, and one fun cocktail; for a bigger crowd, add in red wine and another cocktail choice.

1 lemon, halved

4 cups (1 l) tomato juice

2 teaspoons freshly grated horseradish

2 teaspoons A1 Steak Sauce or
Worcestershire sauce

2 teaspoons celery salt

1 teaspoon cayenne pepper

½ teaspoon paprika

Freshly ground black pepper

2 cups (500 ml) vodka

Ice cubes

6 celery ribs with leaves

6 long, thin radish slices

BLOODY MARY SERVES 6

Squeeze the juice from the lemon halves into a large pitcher. Add the tomato juice, horseradish, A1 sauce, celery salt, cayenne, paprika, and a few grinds of black pepper and stir until thoroughly combined. Add the vodka and stir to combine.

Fill 6 rocks glasses or tumblers with ice and pour the vodka mixture over the ice, dividing it evenly. Garnish with the celery ribs and radish slices and serve.

1 tablespoon plus 1 teaspoon coarse
sea salt

2 teaspoons chile powder

5 limes

4 bottles (12 fl oz/375 ml each) Mexican
beer, such as Dos Equis or Pacifico

4 teaspoons Worcestershire sauce

Hot pepper sauce to taste

Ice cubes

MICHELADA SERVES 4

Spread the salt and chile powder on a small, flat plate. Cut 1 lime into 4 wedges. Moisten the rims of 4 tall glasses or tumblers with a lime wedge and dip each rim into the chile salt to coat it evenly. Save the lime wedges for garnish. Juice the remaining 4 limes; you should have about ½ cup (125 ml) of lime juice. In a pitcher, gently stir together the lime juice, beer, Worcestershire sauce, and a shot of hot pepper sauce. Fill the glasses with ice cubes. Pour the michelada into the glasses, garnish each with a lime wedge, and serve.

1½ cups (375 ml) fresh grapefruit juice

1 cup (250 ml) vodka

Ice cubes

4 thinly sliced grapefruit wheels

GREYHOUND SERVES 4

In a pitcher, combine the grapefruit juice and vodka. Fill 4 highball glasses or tumblers with ice and pour the grapefruit mixture over the ice, dividing it evenly. Garnish each glass with a grapefruit slice and serve.

RAMOS GIN FIZZ SERVES 4

1 cup (250 ml) gin

3 tablespoons fresh lemon juice

1 tablespoon fresh lime juice

3 tablespoons sugar

4 pasteurized egg whites

3 tablespoons heavy cream

Orange flower water

3 cups (1 lb/500 g) crushed ice

1⅓ cups (325 ml) club soda

Freshly grated nutmeg or lemon twists for garnish (optional)

In a blender, combine the gin, lemon juice, lime juice, sugar, egg whites, and cream with a splash of orange flower water and the crushed ice. Blend until frothy, about 1 minute.

Divide among 4 highball glasses. Top each one with an equal amount of the club soda. Garnish with nutmeg or lemon, if desired.

MINT MOJITO SERVES 4

Leaves from 1 bunch fresh mint, plus 4 sprigs for garnish

1 tablespoon simple syrup

½ cup (125 ml) fresh lime juice

1 cup (250 ml) golden rum

Crushed ice

4 lime wheels for garnish

In a pitcher, combine the mint leaves, simple syrup, and lime juice and muddle until the mint is broken up. Add the rum and stir until well mixed. Fill 4 highball glasses with ice. Pour the mojito into the glasses, dividing it evenly. Garnish each glass with a lime wheel and a mint sprig and serve.

GINGER SHANDY SERVES 4

3 bottles (330 ml each) chilled Hoegaarden beer

1 bottle (12 fl oz/375 ml) chilled ginger beer

1 thinly sliced lemon

Fresh mint sprigs

Crushed ice

In a large pitcher, combine the Hoegaarden beer with the ginger beer. Stir in half of the lemon slices and mint sprigs to taste. Fill 4 tall glasses with ice. Add the remaining lemon slices to the glasses and pour in the shandy, dividing it evenly. Garnish each drink with a mint sprig and serve.

Authentic Lone Star–style chili is all about meat—beef only—and heaps of ancho chile powder, with the true Texan cook eschewing the beans found in chili pots elsewhere in the country. You can make the chili up to 3 days in advance, which leaves you time to bake up some corn bread before the day of the game.

TEXAS BEEF CHILI SERVES 8

Heat a frying pan over medium heat. Add the cumin seeds and heat, stirring often, until toasted (you may see a wisp of smoke), about 1 minute. Transfer to a mortar and finely grind with a pestle (or use a spice grinder). Transfer to a bowl and add the chile powder, paprika, and oregano. Mix well and set aside.

Cut the beef into ½-inch (12-mm) cubes. Season with salt and pepper. In a Dutch oven or heavy-bottomed pot over medium-high heat, warm 2 tablespoons of the oil. In batches to avoid crowding, add the beef cubes and cook, turning occasionally, until browned, about 5 minutes per batch. Transfer to a plate.

Add the remaining 1 tablespoon oil to the pot. Add the onion, jalapeño, bell pepper, and garlic and reduce the heat to medium. Cover and cook, stirring occasionally, until the onion softens, about 5 minutes. Uncover, add the spice mixture, and stir well for 30 seconds. Stir in the beer and broth. Return the beef to the pot, cover, and reduce the heat to low. Simmer until the beef is fork-tender, 1½–2 hours.

Remove the chili from the heat and let stand for 5 minutes. Skim off any fat that rises to the surface. Return the pot to medium heat and bring to a simmer. Transfer about ½ cup (125 ml) of the cooking liquid to a small bowl, add the cornmeal, and whisk well. Stir into the chili and cook until lightly thickened, about 1 minute.

Season to taste with salt and pepper. Spoon the chili into warmed bowls and serve hot, with bowls of Cheddar, onions, sour cream, and jalapeños on the side for sprinkling on top.

2 teaspoons whole cumin seeds

¼ cup (1 oz/30 g) ancho chile powder

1 tablespoon Spanish smoked paprika

2 teaspoons dried oregano

4 lb (2 kg) boneless beef chuck roast

Kosher salt and freshly ground pepper

3 tablespoons olive oil

1 large yellow onion, chopped

1 jalapeño chile, seeded and chopped

1 large red bell pepper, seeded and chopped

4 cloves garlic, chopped

1 bottle (12 oz/375 ml) lager beer

1 cup (250 ml) beef broth or water

2 tablespoons yellow cornmeal

Shredded Cheddar cheese, chopped red onions, sour cream, and minced jalapeño chiles for serving

A grilled cheese sandwich, with its crunchy exterior and melting center, is comfort food at its best. Since it's composed of just a few simple ingredients, seek out good-quality farmhouse Cheddar, applewood-smoked bacon, and the juiciest tomatoes you can find.

CHEDDAR, BACON & TOMATO PANINI MAKES 2 PANINI

4 thick-cut slices applewood-smoked bacon, halved crosswise

4 slices country-style bread

¼ lb (125 g) sharp farmhouse Cheddar cheese, thinly sliced

4 thick slices ripe tomato, drained on paper towels

2 tablespoons unsalted butter, at room temperature

In a large frying pan over medium heat, fry the bacon until crisp and brown, about 8 minutes. Transfer to paper towels to drain. Discard the fat in the pan.

Lay two of the bread slices on a work surface and top each with one-fourth of the cheese, 2 slices of tomato, half of the bacon, and the remaining cheese. Top with the remaining two bread slices. Spread the top and bottom of each sandwich with ½ tablespoon of the butter.

Return the frying pan to medium heat. Add the sandwiches. Place a flat lid or a heatproof plate on the sandwiches to weight them down. Cook until the undersides are golden brown and the cheese starts to melt, about 2 minutes. Flip the sandwiches, weight them down with the lid, and brown the other sides, about 2 minutes longer. Cut each sandwich in half (or quarters) and serve right away.

Pull this grown-up mac and cheese from the oven—bubbling hot with its gooey sauce of fontina and Cheddar and its buttery crown of crisp bread crumbs—and you'll never return to store-bought. Bake it in individual ramekins or a full-size baking dish.

MACARONI & CHEESE CUPS SERVES 12

In a large frying pan, melt 3 tablespoons of the butter over medium-low heat. Add the garlic and cook, stirring frequently, until tender but not browned, about 3 minutes. Add the bread crumbs and stir until coated with butter. Set aside.

Preheat the oven to 350°F (180°C). Butter twelve 6-oz (180-ml) ramekins or a shallow 3-quart (3-l) baking dish.

Bring a large pot of lightly salted water to a boil over high heat. Add the macaroni and stir occasionally until the water returns to a boil. Cook according to the package directions until not quite al dente. (The macaroni will cook again in the oven, so do not overcook it now.) Drain well and set aside.

Add the remaining 4 tablespoons (2 oz/60 g) butter to the pot used for the pasta and melt over medium heat. Whisk in the flour. Reduce the heat to medium-low and let bubble for 1 minute without browning. Gradually whisk in the milk, raise the heat to medium, and bring to a boil, whisking frequently. Remove from the heat and stir in the cheeses along with the mustard. Season with salt and pepper. Stir in the pasta. Spread in the prepared ramekins or baking dish and sprinkle evenly with the buttered bread crumbs.

Bake until the crumbs are browned and the sauce is bubbling, about 20 minutes. Let cool for 5 minutes, then serve hot.

7 tablespoons (3½ oz/105 g) unsalted butter, plus more for the baking dish

1 clove garlic, minced

1½ cups (3 oz/90 g) coarse fresh bread crumbs

Kosher salt and freshly ground pepper

1 pound (500 g) elbow macaroni, penne, ziti, or mostaccioli

¼ cup (1½ oz/45 g) all-purpose flour

3 cups (750 ml) whole milk, warmed

2 cups (8 oz/250 g) shredded sharp Cheddar cheese

2 cups (8 oz/250 g) shredded fontina cheese

½ teaspoon dry mustard

BASIC RECIPES

ALL-PURPOSE BBQ RUB

MAKES ABOUT ⅔ CUP (5 OZ/160 G)

¼ cup (2 oz/60 g) granulated sugar

1 tablespoon firmly packed
golden brown sugar

¼ cup (1 oz/30 g) paprika

1 tablespoon chile powder

1 teaspoon cayenne pepper

1 teaspoon smoked paprika

Kosher salt and freshly ground
black pepper

In a small container with a tight-fitting lid, stir together the sugars, paprika, chile powder, cayenne, smoked paprika, 1 teaspoon salt, and several grinds of pepper. Cover and shake vigorously to mix.

Use right away or store in a cool, dark place for up to 1 month.

BLUE CHEESE DIP

MAKES ABOUT 3 CUPS (750 G)

1 cup (8 oz/250 g) sour cream

¼ cup (60 ml) mayonnaise

1 tablespoon Worcestershire sauce

1 tablespoon fresh lemon juice

1 teaspoon steak sauce

2 cloves garlic, finely minced, then
crushed to a paste

2 tablespoons chopped fresh chives

⅛ teaspoon cayenne pepper

1 cup (5 oz/155 g) crumbled blue cheese

Kosher salt and freshly ground black
pepper

In a bowl, combine the sour cream, mayonnaise, Worcestershire sauce, lemon juice, steak sauce, garlic, chives, and cayenne and stir until well mixed. Fold in the cheese and season with salt and pepper.

Cover and refrigerate until ready to serve, or for up to 3 days. The dip tastes best if made a day ahead.

HOMEMADE KETCHUP

MAKES ABOUT 1½ CUPS (375 G)

1 can (28 oz/875 g) crushed Roma
tomatoes

¼ cup (1¼ oz/40 g) light corn syrup

3 tablespoons cider vinegar

2 tablespoons minced yellow onion

2 tablespoons minced red bell pepper

1 small clove garlic, minced

1 tablespoon firmly packed
golden brown sugar

1 teaspoon kosher salt

⅛ teaspoon freshly ground pepper

Pinch *each* of ground allspice, ground
cloves, celery seeds, and yellow mustard
seeds

½ bay leaf

In a heavy saucepan over medium heat, combine all of the ingredients. Bring to a boil, stirring. Reduce the heat to medium-low and cook at a brisk simmer, stirring frequently, until the mixture thickens and has reduced by half, about 1 hour.

Rub the ingredients through a medium-mesh sieve into a heatproof

bowl, discarding any solids. Let cool. Transfer to a covered container and refrigerate overnight to allow the flavors to blend before using. Use right away or refrigerate for up to 2 weeks.

CLASSIC BBQ SAUCE

MAKES ABOUT 2 CUPS (500 G)

1 cup (8 oz/250 g) ketchup

2 tablespoons yellow mustard

1 tablespoon cider vinegar

2 teaspoons firmly packed dark brown
sugar

½ cup (125 ml) low-sodium chicken broth

Kosher salt and freshly ground pepper

2 chipotle chiles in adobo sauce,
finely chopped (optional)

¼ teaspoon ground cumin (optional)

In a saucepan over medium heat, combine the ketchup, mustard, vinegar, brown sugar, broth, a pinch of salt, and 2 teaspoons pepper. Bring to a simmer, stirring to dissolve the sugar. For a Southwest-style sauce, stir in the chiles and cumin. Simmer for 5 minutes for a relatively thin sauce or for 10–15 minutes for a thick sauce. Season to taste with salt. Use right away or let cool, cover, and refrigerate for up to 1 month.

BASIC SHRIMP BRINE

MAKES ABOUT 6 CUPS (1.5 L), OR
ENOUGH FOR 2 LB (1 KG) SHRIMP

½ cup (4 oz/125 g) kosher salt

2 tablespoons sugar

1 teaspoon ground cumin

1 teaspoon ground coriander

In a large bowl, combine 6 cups (1.5 l)
water, the salt, sugar, cumin, and
coriander and stir to dissolve the
salt and sugar. Use right away.

ROMESCO SAUCE

MAKES ABOUT 3 CUPS (750 G)

4 slices coarse country bread, crusts
removed and bread torn into chunks

6 tablespoons (90 ml) red wine vinegar

⅔ cup (3 oz/90 g) slivered almonds

2 cloves garlic

½ cup (3½ oz/105 g) canned diced
tomatoes with juice

2 canned roasted piquillo peppers,
drained

2 teaspoons smoked paprika

Kosher salt

½ cup (125 ml) extra-virgin
olive oil

Place the bread chunks in a bowl, add
the vinegar, toss to coat, and let soften
for about 10 minutes. In a small, dry
frying pan over medium heat, toast
the almonds, stirring, until just golden,
about 5 minutes. Transfer to a plate
and let cool completely.

Drop the garlic cloves into a food
processor with the motor running
and process until the pieces stop
moving. Add the almonds and pulse
until grainy. Add the bread-and-

vinegar mixture, tomatoes with juice,
peppers, paprika, and ½ teaspoon
salt and process until smooth. With
the motor running, add the oil in a
slow, steady stream and process just
thoroughly mixed. Taste and adjust
the seasoning. Cover and refrigerate
for at least 1 hour or up to 3 days.
Bring to room temperature or warm
before serving.

CREAMY CILANTRO DRESSING

MAKES ABOUT 1 CUP (250 ML)

1 cup (1 oz/30 g) tightly packed fresh
cilantro leaves

½ cup (125 g) sour cream

¼ cup (60 ml) olive oil

Juice of 2 limes

1 small clove garlic

Kosher salt

In a blender or food processor,
combine the cilantro, sour cream,
oil, lime juice, and garlic and process
until smooth. Season to taste with salt.

STROMBOLI DOUGH

MAKES 2 BALLS OF DOUGH

3⅓ cups (13½ oz/425 g) all-purpose
flour, plus more for dusting

¼ cup (1 oz/30 g) whole-wheat flour

1 package (2¼ teaspoons) quick rise
yeast

1 tablespoon sugar

1 tablespoon kosher salt

1¼ cups (300 ml) warm water
(110°F/43°C), plus more as needed

2 tablespoons olive oil,
plus more as needed

In a food processor, combine the
flours, yeast, sugar, and salt and pulse
to mix. With the motor running, add
the warm water and the 2 tablespoons
oil in a steady stream, then pulse
until the dough comes together in a
rough mass, about 12 seconds.
If the dough does not come together,
sprinkle with 1–2 teaspoons more
water and pulse again until a rough
mass forms. Let the dough rest for
5–10 minutes. Process again, until
the dough is tacky to the touch but
not sticky, 25–30 seconds. Transfer
to a lightly floured work surface
and knead until the dough is smooth
and elastic, 3–4 minutes. Form into
a smooth ball. Place in a large oiled
bowl, turn the dough to coat in oil,
and cover with plastic wrap. Let the
dough rise in a warm place until
doubled in bulk, about 1½ hours.
Cut the dough in half, place one half
on a floured work surface for making
the stromboli and reserve the other
half for future use. (Reserved dough
should be placed in a lock-top plastic
bag. Refrigerate for up to 1 day or
freeze for up to 1 month; bring to
room temperature before using.)

INDEX

FAN FARE

Conceived and produced by Weldon Owen, Inc.
In collaboration with Williams Sonoma, Inc.
3250 Van Ness Avenue, San Francisco, CA 94109

A WELDON OWEN PRODUCTION

1150 Brickyard Cove Road
Richmond, CA 94801
www.weldonowen.com

Copyright © 2017 Weldon Owen, Inc.
and Williams Sonoma, Inc.
All rights reserved, including the right of
reproduction in whole or in part in any form.

Printed in China

10 9 8 7 6 5 4 3 2 1

Library of Congress Cataloging-in-Publication
data is available.

ISBN: 978-1-68188-627-5

WELDON OWEN, INC.

President & Publisher Roger Shaw
SVP, Sales & Marketing Amy Kaneko

Associate Publisher Amy Marr
Senior Editor Lisa Atwood

Creative Director Kelly Booth
Art Director Marisa Kwek
Designer Alexandra Zeigler
Senior Production Designer Rachel Lopez Metzger

Associate Production Director Michelle Duggan
Imaging Manager Don Hill

Photographer Lauren Burke
Food Stylist Lillian Kang
Prop Stylist Claire Mack

ACKNOWLEDGMENTS

Weldon Owen wishes to thank the following people for their generous support
in producing this book: Jackson Barlow, Lesley Bruynesteyn, Olivia Caminiti,
David Gantz, Veronica Laramie, Alexis Mersel, and Elysa Weitala.